PEOPLE SUCK

A Cheat Code for Introverts

Mark Drolsbaugh

Cover design and layout by KillerCovers.com

All stories and anecdotes feature people who were personally interacted with and interviewed. With the exception of a few people who gave permission to use their actual names, most names and identifying details have been altered in the interest of privacy.

This book is an educational and informational resource. While every effort has been made to provide current and accurate information, the publisher cannot guarantee the outcome of any recommendations provided herein.

ISBN: 978-1-7326094-3-3

Library of Congress Control Number: 2022944165

Published by:
Handwave Publications
P.O. Box 45
1851 West Point Pike
West Point, PA 19486

Dedication

To those of you who thought it was your job to be someone else.
Honor the Real You.

TABLE OF CONTENTS

Foreword

*Several famous introverts were invited to write the foreword.
None of them showed up.*

INTRODUCTION

This was an easy book to write. Because I write at home, where I like it. The hard part comes when someone asks, *"would you be willing to do a presentation about your book?"*

That's when the alarm bells go off in my head.

A presentation? In front of a few hundred people? Why would an introvert want to do that?

Of course, being the people pleaser that I am, I say yes. And then I start mentally berating myself.

What are you doing, Drolz? You're a hot mess in large crowds. Why did you willingly agree to put yourself in front of another one?

As the date of the presentation comes closer and closer, I become obsessed. I prepare. And overprepare. Outlines are written, notes are compiled, and I rehearse. Repeatedly. Over and over, in search of elusive perfection.

I'm not the only one who does this. Chris Rock, who is also an introvert, rehearses six months for a one-hour comedy special. Of course, he goes out there and nails it. Then he's gone. Poof! Outta there.

When I wrote my first book, *Deaf Again,* it wasn't because I wanted to be an author. I wrote it because I wanted people to understand what it means to be deaf. I had struggled with my deaf identity for a long time, and most of this struggle was unnecessary. Being deaf in and of itself was not the issue. It was lack of awareness, on so many levels, that made life difficult. Writing a book about it was my way of saying *it doesn't have to be that way.*

Many people have no idea what it means to be deaf, so I vented.

No one gets it. People suck!

And then a funny thing happened.

After *Deaf Again* was published, other deaf people appeared out of nowhere—either in person or via email—and floored me with their responses.

"That's exactly how I felt."

"I thought I was the only one."

"My family wouldn't listen to me. I showed them your book, and now they get it."

"Oh. My. God. It's like we're the same person."

"Thank you. You gave me license to be me."

Writing about the deaf experience turned out to be rewarding in an entirely different way than initially expected. One of the underlying messages:

We can't always change the way others perceive us. But we can change the way we perceive ourselves. And we must embrace ourselves for who we truly are.

That was a powerful experience. It was time to move on.

Or so I thought.

Several years later, I ranted on Facebook about common misconceptions, ignorance, and all those people who just don't get it.

But this rant had nothing to do with being deaf. I had merely shared my frustration as an introvert. A lot of people have no idea what it means to be an introvert, so I vented.

No one gets it. People suck!

And then a funny thing happened.

After that infamous Facebook rant, other introverts appeared out of nowhere—either in the comments section, in person, or via email—and floored me with their responses.

"I'm the same way."

"You're not the only one."

"It's like we're clones."

"People don't understand that I have to recharge."

"A good TV show and a glass of wine is all I need."

I was surprised at how many people said that they, too, preferred a good book over a night on the town. What hit me was how so many of these people appeared to be anything but introverted. I wouldn't have known if they hadn't told me.

But there's one big difference: as a deaf person, I'm empowered. I face ignorance every now and then, but I know how to advocate for my rights. As an introvert, I get weird looks when I try to explain myself. I still struggle in a world that's biased toward extroverts.

It doesn't have to be that way.

PART I
IT'S COMPLICATED

HOW TO USE THIS BOOK

When this book was in the early stages of completion, some people expressed concern about the title and content.

"People Suck? Are you serious? How many people do you want to alienate with that?"

Just for the record, I'm not an angry grandpa shouting at kids to get off my lawn. I cherish every individual person in my life.

Groups, on the other hand, are more complicated. Introverts can and do enjoy larger gatherings, but only to a certain extent. There are times when we're fine with it, and there are times when we need a break. And then there are times when we suck it up, going against the grain of who we are, because we feel pressure to conform.

Sometimes the pressure gets to us and we feel burned out. It's nothing personal. We just need some alone time.

Besides, if you do an Internet search for "people suck," you'll find some pretty cool t-shirts and coffee mugs.

As for the content of *People Suck*, there were some reservations as well.

"How are you going to help any introverts? Good luck getting them out of the house."

One of the cool t-shirts has a solution for that:

Introverts Unite—Separately in Your Own Homes.

But seriously, is this book really going to *help* anyone?

Does it need to?

There's an introvert page on Facebook called *Understanding Introverts.* The conversations and jokes are eye-opening. One of the themes that struck me was the constantly-posed question:

Who said that introverts have to change?

That got the gears in my head spinning. Why are there so many books and self-help articles for introverts? Why isn't there an article titled *An Extrovert's Survival Guide: How to Think Before You Speak* or even *Calm the Fuck Down: An Extrovert's Guide to Relaxing Vacation Getaways?*

I thought I had the answer to the above questions:

We're outnumbered.

It's an extrovert-dominated world. It's the outspoken extrovert who often gets the promotion because he tooted his own horn. Introverts aren't fond of tooting.

It's more complicated than that.

Most articles and books will tell you that introverts are in the minority, and my initial research indicated 25% to 40% of the population is introverted. But something gnawed at me.

While tossing around ideas for this book, I asked some of my more extroverted friends for feedback. A lot of times, they wound up saying, *"waitaminute. That's not exclusive to introverts. I'm the same way."*

Many of them insisted that they, too, wanted nothing more than to plop down on the couch after a tough week at work. They, too, had no patience for meetings that could have been an email. They, too, preferred working from home.

Could it be that they, too, are also introverts? At least to some degree?

Our society rewards extroverted behavior. It's possible that many of us are actually introverts who put on an extroverted mask, go to the old nine-to-five, and then crash at the end of the day.

I dug deeper into my research. *A-ha.*

According to *Introvert Power* by Laurie Helgoe, Ph.D., data from the *MBTI Manual* indicated introverts comprised of 50.7% of a significant sample size. A more recent sample in the *MBTI Step II Manual* had it at 57%. There may be more of us than initially thought.

Who knows what the exact numbers are. But I can say without a doubt that there's a *perception*. We perceive the world as more extroverted because of a value system that promotes extroverted behaviors.

But again, that begs the question: *do we have to change? As if we owe anyone anything because our personal traits don't match someone else's ideal?*

You don't owe anyone anything.

Take this book for what it is. A guide. Not an obligation to change. It has tips and strategies on how to coexist with extroverts. There are simple, refreshing ways you can keep being you without compromising your authentic self.

You can read this book from front to back, or you can jump to whichever chapters appeal to you. You can also refer back to the cheat code at the end of the book anytime. Apply whatever is useful.

Enjoy.

WIPEOUT ON A NEW WAVE

As a teenager in the early 1980s, my progressive sensorineural hearing loss took me from hard of hearing to flat-out deaf. It became much harder to socialize with my hearing friends and classmates.

Note: Those who are members of the signing deaf community are not too fond of labels such as "hearing loss" and "hearing impaired." These terms have a negative slant, zeroing in on the ears and ignoring the Whole Person. As someone who later became part of the deaf community, I understand that. At the same time, for those of us who are late-deafened (as I am) or are not members of the deaf community, it can and does feel like a hearing loss.

There was one thing I had that many other late-deafened teenagers didn't. Deaf parents. My parents understood my struggle. They knew I was drowning in the hearing world. They threw me a lifeline.

"We're going to a special event next Sunday," my mom told me. "There's a deaf teenage social club called The New Wave. It meets once a month. You'll feel much better meeting other deaf kids just like you."

It's supposed to be that simple?

We showed up at the event the following Sunday. My mom dropped me off.

"Left me to fend for myself" is more like it.

I looked around and initially, I was pleasantly surprised. Everyone communicated in sign language. For the first time in a long time, I was in a group situation where I could clearly understand what everyone said. Up until that point, I could only manage one-on-one conversations. But on this day, everyone's words were crystal clear.

A new world had opened. For once, I was in a place where I belonged.

Or so I thought.

The level of access I had, compared to events where I was the only deaf person, was off the charts. But there was one problem.

I ran out of stuff to say.

How messed up is that? My parents went out of their way to find a group of people who were exactly like me, and I responded by turning into a wallflower.

I was okay with the two people I actually knew at the event. The other 30 people? Not so much. There was a lot of small talk and it made me uncomfortable.

Yes, it's a beautiful day. The sun is shining and there's not a cloud to be seen for miles. Yes, a thunderstorm will move in tomorrow. It was on the news. Yes, the Phillies won yesterday. That was also on the news. Why is everyone talking about stuff we already know?

I was like Lieutenant Commander Data, the naive android in *Star Trek: The Next Generation.* Data was always fascinated with human nature, but struggled to emulate it. And there I was, doing exactly the same thing. Wanting to belong, but having no idea how.

Some people tried to get a conversation going with me, but I was like a turtle that stuck its head back into its shell. Anytime someone asked a question, I responded with a simple yes or no. I didn't have the ability to reply with something that kept the conversation going.

It's a game of verbal volleyball, and I suck at volleyball.

For whatever reason, I felt like I was supposed to say something deep or meaningful. I could not fathom a whole conversation of small talk. It's like when I first got access to music lyrics thanks to captioning and the Internet. I was in for a shocking surprise.

Whenever I saw a band playing in front of a large, enthusiastic crowd, I figured that band must be singing stuff that's *really deep,* because... *look at that crowd! They're going nuts!* But it was not what I thought it was.

The first time I got a glimpse of the lyrics to several rock songs, I was... disappointed. There was a lot of *yeah yeah yeah* and *baby baby baby* with some *I gotta have you so bad* sprinkled in.

That's it? Seriously? There's got to be more to it than this.

One exception: Prince. That guy just blew me away. The metaphors in his lyrics were, and always will be, pure genius. It took me a moment to figure out that *Little Red Corvette* wasn't really about a car. Brilliant!

But there was no genius at this party. I stood there like a moron. I was in this place where I fit in perfectly with everyone around me, yet I couldn't hold a conversation. I wanted to go home.

The kicker? Thirty years later, I bumped into Sharon, who was there at that New Wave event. Three decades after the fact, my social skills had improved enough to the point where I could talk with her for more than two minutes. So of course, she mentioned the New Wave group. I cringed, not wanting to go back there.

"I remember seeing you at that get-together," Sharon said. "You didn't say much."

"Yes, I remember seeing you there," I confirmed.

"You looked like you didn't want to be there," Sharon continued.

She wasn't wrong. And then she dropped the hammer.

"It seemed like you thought you were better than us."

"Yeah, I know—wait. *What?*"

"You barely said a word. Like you couldn't be bothered."

"Oh, god, no. I was *lost* in that group. I had no idea what to say."

We laughed it off and all was good. But the realization hit me hard: as a teenager, I had unknowingly given off a vibe that said *unapproachable.*

In retrospect, I learned a valuable lesson.

Do the little things that build relationships. And while you're at it, be genuine.

If you show up at an event somewhere, smile when you make eye contact. If you feel awkward, say so. There's no shame in it. If anything, that'll break the ice. I wish I could go back in time, because here's the perfect conversation that never happened:

"Hi, I'm Sharon."

"I'm Mark. Nice to meet you."

Said with eye contact, a polite smile, and handshake.

"What brings you here?"

"My mom. She dropped me off ten minutes ago. It's awkward. I'm a flaming introvert and have no idea what to say to anyone."

"You're funny. Come with me. I'll introduce you to my friends."

Keep being you, and let things flow naturally. One small step at a time.

DUMB STUFF I HAVE DONE

Prior to writing this book, an advisor recommended bouncing a few ideas off some trusted friends and colleagues. One of the people I consulted with was on the fence. He said I might have a unique story angle, but cautioned that "this topic has been written about to death."

That's true. There are a ton of introvert-related books and articles out there.

Is this book overkill, or does the number of resources reflect a high demand?

I turned inward. I looked at my own behavior and decided that yes, this book had to happen. I've done some dumb stuff. There have been times when extroverts questioned what I was doing, and there have been times when even I questioned what I was doing. It warrants a closer look.

Here's an example:

One day, as I pulled into the parking lot of my favorite convenience store, I saw a familiar face. It was my son's former elementary school teacher. Not just his former elementary school teacher, but his *favorite* elementary school teacher. I hadn't seen him in eight years.

Seeing this teacher made me immediately wax nostalgic. That teacher is one of the great ones whose lessons extend far beyond the classroom. He's a man of great character. Many of the life lessons my son learned have come from this guy. It's a gift to have such a great mentor and role model.

As I saw the teacher walking toward the store, I was overcome by a wave of gratitude. I truly appreciate the profound impact he has had on my son. It would be so great to say hello after all these years and say the *thank you* this man so greatly deserves.

So I kept driving. To another store ten minutes away.

Because dammit, I just want my coffee. There's no way I'm getting into a 20-minute conversation at a convenience store.

There's more.

This sequence has happened more than once:

"Hey, Drolz, we're getting together at the pub tonight. You in?"

"Sure, why not."

I don't show up.

The following week, the guys get together again at the pub. Without me.

"Hey!" I protest. "How come no one invites me anywhere?"

I don't deny this seemingly irrational behavior. I've done it. A lot of introverts have done it. There are just times when we need to *shut it down* and it doesn't go over well with society at large.

Just to be clear: it's not them, it's me. This is not a cliché. It's really me. It might be my need to recharge. Or it might be my lack of preparedness. I don't like being caught off guard or having to change plans at the last minute. My introvert brain doesn't process surprises that well.

That teacher I drove away from? I would have verbally stumbled all over myself if I said hello. *I have since mentally prepared a thank you speech for the next time we cross paths. I'm ready for him now.*

Here's one that won't go over well with my wife, Melanie. She has long suspected that I avoid the phone. I have long denied it.

She's right.

We're deaf. We use a videophone. Introverts are already averse to unexpected, random phone calls where you have no idea what the person on the other line wants.

With videophones, you actually have to *look* at that person.

Not good.

There have been times when I walked into our home office, sat at the desk, and started working on one thing or the other. Then the light on the videophone goes off like a disco ball at Studio 54.

I get the hell out of there.

"Why didn't you answer the phone?" Melanie asks.

"Someone called? I was in the bathroom," I shrug.

Melanie rarely reads any of my books. I'm taking a huge risk by assuming she's not going to read this one, either.

I do it with the neighbors, too. I actually love them. They're the nicest folks on the planet. We always say hello, bake cookies for each other, and all that other stuff good neighbors do. But again, there are times when I just don't have the ability to engage. If I'm in recharge mode, I don't talk much. And just like with the phone, sometimes I'll go out of my way to avoid an interaction.

This is normal for introverts. But when you're on a riding mower, it gets comical.

The guys on my street have this synchronized internal clock where we all seem to go out and mow the lawn at exactly the same time on the same day. It's uncanny.

I don't mind saying hello. But if we're all mowing at the same time, there are going to be several moments when we pass each other as we ride our mowers up and down our respective lawns.

To the neighbors, this isn't a big deal at all. For me, it feels awkward. There have been times when I've stepped outside with the intent to mow the lawn, only to do a complete about-face when I notice some other neighbors are already out there. I go back into the house and do something else.

There have also been times when I was the first one out in the yard, and then other neighbors came out a short time afterward. When that happens, I try my best to limit the interaction to one simple *how ya doing*. I even mow in a specific pattern to keep the interaction to a minimum. I call it the Drolz Maneuver. I think the neighbors have noticed.

"Is Mark okay? He's been mowing in circles for ten minutes."

There are times when I genuinely wonder if there's something wrong with me. I'm always relieved to find out I'm not the only one when it comes to puzzling introvert behavior. There's a great article online titled *6 'Weird' Things Introverts Do That Are Actually Completely Normal* by Alena Sidarovich. It can be found in Jenn Granneman's *Introvert, Dear* website. Look it up. A lot of the things Sidarovich shares are similar to what I've just disclosed.

I hope this book likewise delivers a sense of *I'm not the only one* to those who read it.

YOU'RE SO QUIET

Introverts don't like to be in the spotlight. So of course, I flew to Ontario, Canada, and gave a three-hour presentation. Midway through the presentation, the event coordinator asked if I could do a one-hour encore later that afternoon for employees who were unable to attend the morning session.

Another presentation? In front of even more people? Why would I want to do that?

"Absolutely," I said. "Let's go for it."

I had arrived in Canada on a Wednesday evening, gave two presentations on Thursday, and hopped on a flight back to Philadelphia immediately afterward. On Friday, I returned to my day job as a high school guidance counselor.

Soon after returning to work, our school's support staff had to participate in an accreditation interview.

The interviewer opened by asking us to explain our roles within the school. As always, my mind went into overdrive trying to come up with a good answer.

Many introverts struggle to come up with a good answer on a moment's notice. We're the masters of the 4:00am perfect response. But in real time? Not so much. We have to let our thoughts percolate for a while.

The gears in my mind continued to churn. The lights were on, but no one was home. At that moment another person from my department raised her hand. Her response hit the nail on the head. She summarized our roles in less than a minute. It was the mother of all elevator speeches. Another team member chipped in with a few more points for good measure. *Game, set, match.* That's when I knew there was nothing further to say.

I glanced to my right and noticed that there were people from other departments who had yet to say anything. I glanced at the clock. There were only 20 minutes left.

To recap: my colleagues had said it all. There was no need for me to say something just for the sake of saying something. There were at least two other departments that hadn't spoken yet, and time was running out. I decided to keep my mouth shut.

I leaned back in my chair, satisfied that my team had represented itself well. I felt confident that our school would ace the accreditation (we did).

After the meeting was over, a colleague approached me as we walked back to the main building. It was Kevin, who also happened to be a good friend

"Drolz!" Kevin exclaimed. "You were so *quiet.*"

I shrugged and gave him an evasive answer.

"I'm a board member of an organization that has ties to the accreditation team," I replied.

That was true.

"I figured it was best to avoid a conflict of interest."

That was a load of horse manure.

I've known Kevin for more than 25 years. He would have been fine with it if I told him the truth:

"I'm an introvert. If there's no need for me to say anything, I won't."

Yet somehow, in the spur of the moment, I instinctively put up a facade. I'd been conditioned to believe that we have a responsibility to behave like extroverts in the workplace.

It wasn't over yet. As I returned to my office, I crossed paths with Jeff, an administrator from another department.

"Hi Mark," said Jeff. "What was going on back there? You were so *quiet.*"

This time around, I didn't evade the subject.

"What can I say," I smiled. "I'm an introvert."

It felt so good to get that out.

"My team nailed it," I continued. "There was no need to add anything. Besides, I'm not kidding about being an introvert. I need more time to prepare for meetings like this."

Jeff nodded. He seemed to know where I was coming from.

"I'm somewhat of an introvert myself," he acknowledged.

Say what? Jeff is a mover and shaker in our community. I've seen him effortlessly run board meetings. He's given presentations in front of thousands of people. He's calm, cool, and collected. I, on the other hand, am a nervous wreck before I go on stage. I admitted as much.

"It happens to me, too," Jeff confessed. "You're right. We need to prepare in advance. As long as we do that, everything works out just fine."

Wise words. I smiled, surprised to learn that one of the most visible leaders in our community shared something in common with me. We parted ways and I returned to my office.

Before I could get back to work, another colleague, Marvin, dropped by to say hello.

"Hey, Drolz," he said.

Uh-oh. Here it comes.

"You were so *quiet.*"

This was the third person in less than 30 minutes who had to tell me I was *quiet*. This time, my mouth jumped ahead of my brain.

"Why is everyone saying that?" I asked. "I was on stage in Canada for four hours. *Four hours!* The minute I come home, everyone wants to know why I'm so quiet. Am I supposed to put on a tux and tap dance?"

I could tell by the look on Marv's face that he knew he hit a nerve. I felt like an idiot.

"I'm an introvert," I said, regaining my composure. "I don't like calling attention to myself if I don't have to."

"I understand," Marv replied. "It's interesting, though. I notice you tend to do great in your presentations. Do you enjoy the presentations, but not the Q&A afterward?"

Oh my god. It's like he knows me.

"Yes, that happens," I agreed. "I can get through the presentations. I rehearse for that. I usually wind up having a good time. But for the Q&A, I really want to get out of there. I'm *done*."

Q&A's aren't that bad. Most of the time, a question is related to something I've already written or spoken about. But if a question is way out in left field, or if it's presented in a way that hasn't been asked before, that's when I go into brain lock. Sometimes this involves not having a response available on a moment's notice, because introverts tend to rely on long-term memory. Other times, I might not actually draw a total blank, but I might have multiple responses popping up in my head at the same time. It's like a mental traffic jam. A bottleneck. It takes a while for the introverted brain to spit out an intelligible response to a new question.

Marv grinned. As did I. It feels great when someone else gets it. For many introverts, it often feels like we're *The Only One*. And that we have to put on a facade in public, as I did with Kevin.

But we're not *The Only One*. There are more introverts out there than we're aware of. We just happen to live in a world that favors extroverts. Too many times, introverts wind up being misunderstood.

Take John, for example. John works at a corporation that requires him to interact with people all day long. Working in tech support, he moves from office to office as he assists people with their laptops and computers. Sometimes he works with large groups, including set up and tech assistance for conferences.

There has never been a snafu with a keynote speaker under John's watch. Everyone loves him. To the untrained eye, John's a great guy with a rewarding job.

Only one problem: he's exhausted.

At the end of a successful conference, John often retreats to his office where he recharges. He'll have a late lunch, read a news article or two, or simply sit back in his chair and stare out the window. Alone. This is his cherished quiet time. Only few colleagues know this.

Those who don't know John assume he's an extrovert. He's always talking, cracking jokes, and eager to help anyone who needs tech support. But the average person doesn't understand that if John doesn't get his daily dose of quiet time, *the beast* emerges.

"It caught me by surprise," John confessed. "I had a busy day. But it was a *good* busy day. I got back to my office at 4:30 and sat at my desk. Then Roger showed up. All he did was shoot the breeze. Out of nowhere, he said *'whoa. I'll come back later.'* It turns out I gave him the stink eye without even knowing it. I didn't mean it, but I had nothing left in the tank."

The need to recharge is a common refrain amongst introverts. Perhaps the funniest example comes from Rick, who went into full recharge mode at a party. Rick had effortlessly schmoozed with countless people at a gathering when suddenly, out of nowhere, he disappeared.

"Where did Rick go?" I asked.

"Beats me," said Lauren.

Lauren is Rick's wife. She had no idea regarding her husband's whereabouts.

A few minutes later, another friend, Mike, motioned for me to follow him.

"There he is," said Mike. He pointed toward a private den down the end of the hall.

"Well, I'll be damned," I replied.

Rick was alone in the den. Relaxing with an iced tea and a nice book.

"He's reading a book," Mike chuckled. "At his own party."

Yes. This was Rick's party. At his house. Where he had cooked food, mingled with guests, served drinks, told entertaining stories, and... disappeared. In his own house. To read a book.

"He's an introvert," I replied. "I'm the same way."

Rick will spew his coffee when he reads this. Truth is, he did a brave thing. He hosted a party. That's one of the hardest things an introvert can do. Because if it's your party, you can't leave.

MYTH VS. REALITY

Introverts are a different breed. The way we approach the world, and the way we recharge from it, leads to misunderstandings galore. There are several myths about introverts.

Myth: Introverts don't like to talk.
Reality: Introverts are averse to small talk, but enjoy deep and insightful conversation.

My behavior at the accreditation interview showed that if introverts don't need to say anything, they're not going to. But the key word is *need*. At that meeting, I didn't *need* to talk. Two other colleagues had already spoken, and I was satisfied that they got the job done. Small talk, or repeating things just for the sake of appearances, doesn't appeal to introverts.

But what if something *does* interest us? Our mouths are off to the races. We'll yap until the cows come home. As long as there's passion for an intriguing topic, we're fully engaged.

Introverts are perfectly capable of holding a good conversation. We just don't do it as much as extroverts. We'll step out of our comfort zone every now and then, but for the most part we prefer small groups or individual conversations. And when we do have these conversations, they'll go deep.

Myth: Introverts "choose to be that way."
Reality: We are wired differently. It's not a choice.

I work in a people-oriented job. I'm good at it, but it comes with a cost. That's because each encounter I have with someone at work—no matter how awesome that person is—drains my energy. By the time I get home, I'm worthless. I need a break. It could be in the form of a nap, or it could be parking myself in front of the TV. The nap is the safest option because that's when I can recharge without offending anyone. When I'm in front of the TV, I inadvertently upset my family. They think there's something wrong with me. My wife, Melanie, has no problem letting me know about it. Here's a typical Monday evening conversation in the Drolz household:

"The kids just asked me to order take out," Melanie said. "They asked me because you're giving off a vibe that says *do not disturb.*"

"Aw, crap," I replied. "I'm not in a bad mood or anything. I just need to recharge."

"You *look* like you're in a bad mood."

"I'm not. Just give me 30 minutes. My energy will be back. I promise."

In 30 minutes, my energy *is* back. At which point I can hang out with the kids, play with the dog, and have actual conversations without appearing aloof.

I could be wrong about the dog. Playing with the dog actually recharges me. Perhaps that's why I say hello to her first when I get home.

Anytime an introvert gets called out for their behavior, it's often in a blaming manner.

What's the matter? Why do you choose to be so reclusive?

We don't choose. We are literally *wired this way*. In *The Introvert Advantage: How to Thrive in an Extrovert World* by Marti Olsen Laney, Psy.D., there's a chapter (*The Emerging Brainscape: Born to Be Introverted?*) that describes, in great detail, how an introvert's brain functions differently than an extrovert's. Long story short: introverts are more sensitive to dopamine, and extroverts thrive on it. Dopamine is a type of neurotransmitter that stimulates our motivation to seek rewards and excitement out in the world. Introverts, due to their sensitivity to dopamine, need to take a break when they get overstimulated.

Nonetheless, introverts feel pressure to conform and behave like extroverts. It's what the world expects from us. In *The Introverted Leader: Building on Your Quiet Strength* by Jennifer B. Kahnweiler, Ph.D., there's an exercise intended to show extroverts what it feels like. Kahnweiler asks us to flash the flashiest of smiles, show our teeth, and to hold that smile for at least five seconds. Then she asks how it feels to force a smile in that manner.

She nailed it.

This is precisely what introverts do, several times a day. It's like wearing a mask. We have to put that mask on in certain work or social situations, even when our energy is running low. To counteract this, we need to take breaks and recharge. Again, it's not a choice. It's how we're wired.

Myth: Introverts are shy.
Reality: There's a difference between "shy" and "introverted."

A shy person doesn't feel comfortable interacting with people (especially new people). A shy person uses as few words as possible and wants to retreat. There's a reason it's sometimes called *painfully shy*. This doesn't always apply to introverts.

An introvert may be comfortable interacting with others, although with a preference for smaller groups. An introvert may also struggle to get warmed up with new people, but it's usually because of a disdain for small talk. Once we're warmed up, we can engage in quality conversation.

An introvert can go to parties and even be the life of the party. It's just that we have a finite amount of energy. Inevitably, the introvert needs to step back and recharge. We're not painfully shy, but there will be times when we're painfully exhausted.

Laney made a great analogy in *The Introvert Advantage* when she said extroverts are like solar panels. They gain energy when they're outside. That's definitely not me. As an introvert, I feel like a gas-powered car. Introverts can get out there and zoom down the highway with the best of them. But eventually, we're going to run out of gas.

Myth: Introverts are loners.

Reality: We are so comfortable when we're alone, it looks like we're shutting the world out. But we do, in fact, have a great (and often small) group of quality friends and enjoy doing things with them.

I'm blessed with the greatest group of friends an introvert could ask for. We don't go out much. When we do, it's a usually a group of six to eight people. We may spontaneously get together on some random Friday and not do it again until several months later. At which point it feels like we just saw each other yesterday. We get along great all over again. Then we go our own separate ways until whenever.

Myth: Introverts can't succeed in the extrovert-dominated workplace.

Reality: We have much to offer. Hopefully the extroverts are paying attention.

In the traditional workplace, extroverts are more likely to get promoted because they are visibly out there, being vocal, and utilizing a team approach. That's going to move you up the ladder much faster than the guy crunching numbers in a backroom cubicle.

This doesn't mean that introverts are doomed to a life of eternal pencil-pushing at the office. We have ways of utilizing our strengths. Some of the most successful people on this planet are introverted CEOs and entrepreneurs who broke the mold. If they couldn't fit into the traditional nine-to-five workplace, they kicked the door down and created their own opportunities.

Yes, the world is biased towards extroverts. This doesn't mean that extroverts are better. It's up to us to utilize the strengths that come with being who we are.

COVID-19: A NEW REALITY

When the COVID-19 pandemic hit the world in 2020, life as we knew it was turned upside-down. We were caught unprepared and had to make on-the-fly adjustments as we tried to figure out how to address what was going on.

Before going any further, it needs to be said that COVID-19 should never be described as a blessing in disguise or as having a silver lining. The pandemic is best defined as a tragedy that resulted in the loss of countless lives. Only with that caveat can it be acknowledged that it forced us to take a good look at ourselves. And maybe, just maybe, we learned something.

An interesting subplot formed during the early going. When lockdowns went into effect, a significant portion of the world grew antsy. Restaurants closed. Bars closed. Sports arenas closed. People could no longer get together in ways that were taken for granted for generations.

Extroverts climbed the walls.

Introverts said, *"you're telling us to stay home? Okay."*

It was interesting to watch. Restaurants fought back against the shutdown by adapting their services to include delivery and pickup. Some defiantly stayed open for indoor dining, and they had their share of customers who threw caution to the wind. These customers couldn't bear *not* hanging out at their favorite establishments.

It's the same food no matter whether you eat it at home or on the patio at Joe's Bar and Grill. But there were those who absolutely had to be on that patio, consequences be damned. As an introvert, I found this fascinating.

A vast number of businesses switched to remote work in order to maintain safe social distancing. Again, there was something interesting to observe.

We became more efficient in ways that would make an introvert say *told ya so.*

I wish it didn't take a pandemic for people to notice this. I really do. But it wasn't long before people realized that there were indeed advantages to the introverted lifestyle. Especially when it came to working from home.

Note: I work in the school system, which requires another disclaimer. No matter how much we tout the efficiency of working from home, this doesn't apply to schoolchildren. For them, social interaction at school (and elsewhere) is a developmental necessity that greatly contributes to their overall well-being. They need to be out in the world, not stuck at home with their noses buried in their laptops. Without genuine human interaction, they're not going to thrive.

When schools began shutting down in March 2020, we had no idea what to do. Many schools, mine included, were not prepared for a switch to remote learning. We initially thought we would quarantine for two weeks and then life would go back to normal. It didn't. Weeks soon turned into months. We had to adapt to a new normal.

That's when I noticed something that blew my mind. Simply by staying home—where it was literally a 30-second commute to my home office—I found myself getting more done. A *lot* more. In four hours of work at home, I got more done than I did in eight hours on campus. It reached a point where I could finish a whole week's worth of prep work by Tuesday morning. I was amazed at my newfound productivity. I said as much during an online department meeting.

"But it's not the same," lamented one of my extroverted colleagues. "I miss everyone."

"Are you kidding me?" I replied. "I'm on a roll. For once, I'm ahead of schedule."

When it became obvious that things were not going to return to normal after a few weeks, we did everything we could to make it work. It wasn't the same as far as human interaction goes, but I became fascinated with how we functioned differently. I compared my on-site schedule to my remote schedule. Again, mind-blowing. Here's how it stacked up:

On-site Work Schedule:

- Wake up at 5:55am and cuss at the alarm.
- Shower, brush teeth, get dressed.
- Make breakfast. Get distracted by the dog.
- Take dog for a walk.
- Dog takes its damn time finding a spot to do its business.
- Realization sinks in that I could be late for work.
- Grab briefcase and zoom out the door.
- Realization sinks in that I forgot breakfast. And lunch.
- Pull over at a convenience store.
- Buy greasy breakfast sandwich. And lunch.
- Inhale greasy breakfast sandwich while fighting through traffic.
- Punch in at 7:55am.
- Quick bathroom break thanks to greasy breakfast sandwich.
- Office work, educational support, and walk-in counseling.
- Inhale lunch while preparing for advisory sessions.
- Advisory sessions with high school students.
- Follow-up reports, individual student meetings.

- Staff meetings, emails, phone calls.
- Punch out at 4:00pm, grab briefcase, and zoom out the door.
- Fight through rush hour traffic.
- Pick up the kids at whatever school or sporting event they have.
- Arrive home. Plop down on the couch.
- The kids are hungry. I tell them to order pizza.
- I'm done for day. And I really mean *done.*

Remote Work Schedule

- Wake up at 5:55am and cuss at the alarm.
- Brush teeth. The shower can wait. Who am I trying to impress?
- Walk 30 seconds to my home office.
- Punch in at 6:00am. Yes, two hours early. There's a reason for this.
- Prepare outline of plans for the day.
- Locate and store online materials for later use.
- Prepare and enjoy a nice, healthy breakfast.
- Walk the dog. She can sniff around all she wants.
- Review or create lesson plan for the day.
- Create lesson plans for the rest of the week.
- Feeling kind of funky around 8:00am. Take that shower after all.
- Back to work. Update Planbook with new lesson plans.
- Realization sinks in that I'm way ahead of schedule.
- Healthy snack.
- Virtually assist students with college applications.
- Dog wants to go for another whiz. She loves it when I'm home.
- Review videos and special effects to add to lesson plans.
- Daughter wants a ride to Dunkin' Donuts. Absolutely.
- Answer emails from staff and students.
- Lunch.
- 20-minute walk. This isn't a break. It's an idea-generating activity.
- Jot down ideas and discussion topics from aforementioned walk.
- Virtual advisory sessions with high school students.
- Healthy snack.

- Virtual staff meetings or individual student meetings.
- Follow up reports.
- Professional development course. Quick break every 25 minutes.
- Punch out at 5:00pm.
- Throw something on the grill and enjoy a nice family dinner.
- Enjoy any subsequent evening activities with the family.

See the difference? We've stumbled onto an introvert lifestyle that benefits everyone. Here are some key takeaways from the remote work schedule:

Walking: I lost fifteen pounds doing this. Walking isn't even strenuous. Just do it every day, for 20 or 30 minutes. You'll be surprised at the results. It's true what they say: sitting is the new smoking. Whenever you can, go for a walk.

Clearing the mind: This happens anyway during your daily walk. But if you're not walking, sitting in a quiet room with no distractions will do. As will lying down on the couch. Even doing the dishes will suffice, so long as you're not distracted by the television, radio, or someone else's conversation. When you engage in quiet, meditative activity or rest, you clear your mind. When you clear your mind, you open the floodgates to the most creative ideas you might not have known you have. Your productivity skyrockets.

Hyper-focusing: My extroverted wife makes fun of me for this. She says I suck at multitasking. That's true. But I'm an ace at hyper-focusing. When you zone in on a task, and nothing but that task, you will complete it with laser-like precision. Again, productivity skyrockets.

Taking breaks: Breaks are your friend. Always recharge. If I'm working on something I really love—such as this book—I can go for hours on end without a break. But when it comes to the old nine-to-five, or any other situations where you have to deal with people on a regular basis, your energy can get drained in a short time. Take breaks and you'll find the quality of your work improving. I discovered this by happenstance when I realized my dog's pee schedule was non-negotiable. I built breaks into my schedule with the understanding that while I was actually working, there were to be no interruptions. Some people with an old-school mindset aren't comfortable with the idea of multiple breaks. The new-school response: with regular breaks, your productivity at the end of the day is much higher than it would be with The Old Way of Doing Things.

Healthy food: When you munch on an apple instead of a greasy breakfast sandwich, you can see the difference in your energy level. Which brings us to the length of the work day. When fueled by greasy breakfast sandwiches, I was exhausted by 4:00pm. When eating healthier, I was able to punch out around 5:00pm with plenty of energy left. At which point I'd lift weights in the basement or go for a run.

High Intensity Intervals: At first glance, it looks like I had an 11-hour work day, punching in at 6:00am and punching out at 5:00pm. But I'm not going to take credit for that. Instead, I stretched out the day, fit in numerous breaks, and worked in short, hyper-focused bursts. I later learned that other people had this figured out a long time ago. Look up the Pomodoro Technique. It works.

Before wrapping up this chapter, it needs to be said that all of the above is not the exclusive domain of introverts. I've had conversations with extroverts who told me they now enjoy working remotely. They acknowledge and appreciate the efficiency. They love how the meeting that could have been an email is now, in fact, an email.

PART II
SUCCESS, INTROVERT STYLE

MIND POWER

"Hey Mark," Laura grinned, as she stood at the door to my office. "Am I interrupting anything?"

"No," I replied. "But this is weird. Sharon and I were *just* talking about you."

"We were," Sharon chimed in. "It was like 30 seconds ago."

"Yeah," I nodded. "The same thing happened with Mike last week. I told Sharon about Mike's bowling team and then he—"

"Hi guys," said Mike. He gave a nonchalant wave as he walked past my office.

Laura stared at me in disbelief. Sharon laughed.

"Every time we mention someone, that person shows up," Sharon shrugged. "It's uncanny."

It took Laura a moment to process what had just happened. And then she had an idea.

"Brad Pitt, Brad Pitt, Brad Pitt..."

Brad didn't show up.

But still, there are some things in life that make you go *hmmm.* I tend to notice these things. Especially synchronicities. I wonder if they're just a coincidence or if there's some vibe we send out that subconsciously attracts others. It's like they know, without actually knowing.

My dog does the same thing. All I have to do is just think about going to the fridge and she's pawing at my leg for a snack.

I looked into that Law of Attraction stuff. I've read some books about it.

I really don't know.

Regardless of how much it works, there's still something useful there. Especially for introverts who get lost in their own thoughts.

I need my goals written down. Not necessarily to manifest them. I'm happy if I can just remember them.

It sounds corny, but it's true. You're more likely to accomplish your goals when you write them down. Just about every self-help resource out there recommends it.

There's something in your mind that's activated when you hone your thoughts in a particular manner. Let me explain.

Years ago, after our second child was born, my wife and I realized we had outgrown our Toyota Corolla. It's a nice car that gets nice mileage, but there simply wasn't enough room. We were ready to take the plunge and jump into Suburbia Hell. It was time for... *a minivan.*

I searched online for minivans. There were so many makes, models, and colors.

Did we want a new minivan? A used minivan? A cool-looking minivan (if there is such a thing)? A boring but reliable minivan?

Decisions, decisions.

Being the overthinker that I am, my mind was all minivan, 24/7.

And then it happened.

There were minivans everywhere!

Everywhere we went, we saw one. Or two or three or four.

"Mel! Look! A Kia Sedona. I was just thinking about that."

"Mel! There goes a Honda Odyssey. I just read a review about it."

Mel rolled her eyes as we pulled into a convenience store parking lot.

"What do you think, Mel? Should we stay with Toyota? The Sienna is a little expen—HEY! There it is! Can you believe this? I'm manifesting minivans."

Another eye roll from the wife.

She may have been annoyed, but she'll verify there was a minivan frenzy. There was no shortage of them. The minute I set my mind on them, *poof*, they magically appeared.

Sort of.

They didn't appear out of nowhere. They were always there. It would be more accurate to say that instead of setting my mind on them, I *opened* my mind to them. And that's when I started noticing minivans that had been sharing the road with us all along.

It's the same thing with your goals. If you write them down, you become more aware of what you want. Your mind opens to it. You suddenly find ideas, strategies, and opportunities that help you achieve your goals. They might have slipped by you before, but you'll notice them now.

There's more to it than that. It's not enough to just jot some stuff down on a list. You need to visualize it. You need to *feel* it.

I need to do something extra because my thought process tends to go off the rails. I may have a list of goals right in front of me, but my mind might wander to the list of beers for Larry's Super Bowl party.

We need a better way to get locked in.

And we have one. I swear it works. But first, a little prelude. It might seem a little off the point, but it brings everything together in a powerful way.

In Andrew Leedham's *Unstoppable Self Confidence*, he challenges you to lock in on a positive thought for 15 seconds. He says he learned this from Andy Shaw, the author of *Creating a Bug Free Mind*. He insists it's the most important mental exercise you could ever do.

It doesn't seem like much to ask. It's only 15 seconds of uninterrupted positive thought. That's all. Just 15 seconds.

It's ridiculously hard. It's a mental Mt. Everest.

No worries. I found a cheat code for this cheat code.

First, write a list of goals. Then create a PowerPoint out of it. Make slides with pictures of your dream vacation, the business you've always wanted to open, the front row seats at the ballgame, and any other dream scenario. When you look at those slides, *feel it.* If you're on an exercise program, create a slide with a picture of someone close to your age, someone who has already achieved the fitness goals you want. Look at that picture as if it's you. Again, *feel it.*

Do this every day.

You accomplish several things at once when you do this. You go over your goals on a consistent basis. You stay focused. You open your mind to new opportunities. You feel it. It's a good vibe. Stare at any of the slides for any duration, and you can easily hold 15 seconds of uninterrupted positive thought. You rewire your brain for success.

I know this may sound like claptrap to people who aren't into this kind of thing. But I kept an open mind and tried it. I created a PowerPoint with eight goals in it. These were not easily attainable goals. They're big goals. Within six months, four of those goals happened. Two more are on the horizon and will happen within a year. I'm 100% positive that eventually, all eight goals will be reached.

One of those goals was this book. I rest my case.

Another tip: when you achieve any of the goals you've set, leave them on the PowerPoint. Don't delete. When you go through your goals, the sense of accomplishment you feel for the ones you've already reached spill over to the ones you haven't finished yet. It adds to the sense of *"hey! It's working."* It removes self-doubt. You're allowing your brain to see that your goals are credible.

It doesn't matter if you believe in this or not. If you do it, it'll help. Set clear goals and put them where you can see them. For introverts, especially those of us who tend to overanalyze and get easily distracted, this is an excellent way of staying on track.

A ROLE MODEL FOR INTROVERTS

Pat Croce, the author of *I Feel Great and You Will Too!*, once appeared at a book signing a few miles from my home. It was around that time when Pat was the president and owner of the Philadelphia 76ers. Under his leadership, the 76ers went from last place to the NBA finals. Pat was the spark plug that lit up the whole town.

Obviously, I'm a world-class introvert. I don't just go up to celebrities and talk to them. Had I even attempted to hold a conversation with Pat, I would have babbled incomprehensibly.

I needed a different approach. In the two seconds I met him, I said a quick hello and handed him a letter. The letter was an invitation to attend an event at my school and give a pep talk to our students.

Pat showed up.

The event was a huge success. Pat's energy, as expected, was *electric*. You could feel it all over campus. There was a huge buzz for *weeks* after he left.

Pat is not the poster child for this book.

Then again, who am I to judge? Maybe in private, he's a quiet guy. But when Pat goes out there and does Pat things, he leaves everyone in the dust.

He started out as a physical therapist. When he made it his goal to work in that capacity for the Philadelphia Eagles football team, he literally walked up to the stadium and banged on the door.

They said no.

It didn't matter. Pat walked across the street and banged on another door. He wound up becoming a trainer for both the Philadelphia Flyers hockey team and the 76ers basketball team.

Pat didn't stop there. Always looking for new opportunities, it wasn't long before he owned a chain of fitness centers. Eventually he sold them for $40 million. Soon afterward, he became president and part owner of the 76ers.

That's just who Pat is. If he was the author of this book it would be titled *People Rock: A Cheat Code for Doing Whatever the Hell You Want.*

But regardless of who you are, he did speak one truth that applies to all of us, introverts included. It's right there in his book:

If you don't ask, the answer is always no.

All of us, especially introverts, need to keep this in mind if we want to accomplish more in life.

I know. It's not easy.

Here's an actual conversation I had with my wife:

"Mark, did you apply for the new position they advertised?"

"Nah. It's not my thing."

"Have you ever been promoted?"

"Not really."

"How long have you been working?"

"About 40 years."

"Are you kidding me? Not even *one* promotion?"

"No."

"How many jobs have you had?"

"About seven or eight."

"How many times did you ever get a raise?"

"Many times. My bosses actually like me."

"But no promotion?"

"Never."

"Have you ever *asked* for a promotion?"

"No."

"You're an idiot."

"Nah. I'm an introvert."

Just so you know: had I ever desired a promotion, I would have followed Pat's advice and asked for one. I choose to promote myself in other areas that are more introvert-friendly, such as my writing endeavors. I maintain a balance. I do the best I can within the parameters of my role at work, and keep myself fresh for outside challenges such as writing books and creating websites. Most important, I balance things in such a way that I can have quality time with my family.

But that's just me. If you have that itch to do more, or if you feel stuck where you are, you can create positive change. You don't have to bang on someone's door like Pat did. You can email, text, or post something on social media. Or you can write a letter, like I did.

Oh, and as for that letter I handed to Pat way back when? When he opened it, he wound up reading his own quote: "Hi Pat, you said if we don't ask, the answer is always no. So here I am asking."

Yes, introverts can make things happen. In their own unique way.

DEAL, JUST DEAL

While watching reruns of *Deal or No Deal,* it dawned on me that I'd be a terrible contestant on the show.

I can't help but notice that every contestant talks and talks and talks... but there's no point in talking, because the whole game is based on luck.

The only thing worth talking about during the actual game is mathematical probability. But no, the producers are adept at picking out colorful contestants who will ramble on and on about anything.

"Howie! When I gassed up the car this morning, it cost exactly 24 dollars! And I gassed it up at a 24-hour convenience store! Right around the corner from the church where I got married 24 years ago! I can feel it, Howie! I can feel it in my bones! Case 24!"

Put me on the show. The ratings would plummet.

"Hi, Howie."

"Huh? Nah. Let's get right to it."

"Case 1."

"Case 2."

"Case 3."

"Oh, shit. That wasn't good."

"Case 4."

"Case 5."

"One more? Okay. Case 6."

"What's the offer? Hmmm. That's not my cutoff point. No deal."

At this point, I'd interrupt Howie and ruin the show.

"Howie, let's skip the small talk and make this quick. Ladies, go ahead and open cases 7, 8, 9, 10, and 11."

"No, Howie, I don't need more time. There's no strategy that increases the odds for any particular case. Let's just open those and be done with it."

The cases open and the banker makes an offer.

"Hmmm. The mathematical probability of me leaving with more than that if I keep playing is less than ten percent. I'll take the deal, Howie. I'm outta here."

I'd walk out the door as one of the richest yet most boring contestants ever to grace the set of *Deal or No Deal.*

Am I throwing shade at introverts? As if we're something *less than* the extroverted contestants who make the show so entertaining?

No. We all have our place in this world. Go with your strengths.

So where are the introverts on *Deal or No Deal?*

They're the producers of the show, working behind the scenes without any fanfare. They're the ones calculating which applicants are most likely to boost the ratings.

"That guy's a real screamer. He'll push the ratings through the roof. Howie, he's all yours. Have fun."

And how about that banker? It's an introvert's dream job. You get to work in the shadows. You only have to talk to one person the whole day.

"Hi, Howie. How awesome is it that only you can hear me? Offer the guy $47,000 and send me a drink. I'm doing crossword puzzles in the dark. No, no, I'm not complaining. I love it up here. You keep being you. I'm staying right here where I like it."

INTROVERT LEADERSHIP

Aclass I had signed up for was cancelled at the last minute. I was two credits short of a master's degree. I needed to find something else to replace those missing credits.

As I looked through the course catalog, the only thing available that fit into my schedule was a week-long business course during the summer. I don't remember the name of the course. It had something to do with leadership. And since this course was outside my area of study, I had to meet with the Department Chair to get approval.

"Are you sure you want to do this?" he asked.

"Yes, I'm sure," I replied. "I'm going to be a guidance counselor, but there will be leadership opportunities down the road. I'd like to be prepared for them."

That was in 1994. I'm still a guidance counselor. But hey, I got into that class.

This one-week course met from nine to five every day. That's eight hours of classwork, five days in a row. Up until that point, I'd never attended a class that lasted longer than three hours.

My attention deficit and I were in for a huge challenge.

As I entered the classroom on the first day, my jaw dropped.

"*You?* Uh, hi!" I said, to the imposing figure sitting right next to me.

It was my PE teacher from undergraduate school. My no-nonsense, tough as nails, take no shit from anyone PE teacher. The one who almost flunked me over an unexcused absence. She was right there. In my class. Sitting right next to me. She...

She turned out to be one of the nicest people I've ever known.

Outside of her role as PE teacher, she was an entirely different person. This was the first of many important lessons I learned in my leadership class.

In the past, I often assumed that no-nonsense types—usually teachers and coaches—were mean people who didn't give a rat's ass about you. Nothing could be further than the truth. A lot of times, these no-nonsense types are more invested in your personal growth than in being your friend. They're rooting for you.

As the other students filed in, I noticed that they weren't just any other students. They were employees of the college where I had earned my bachelor's degree. One of them was from the finance office. Another was an administrative professional who worked directly with some of the biggest names on campus. Another was a systems administrator.

These were long-time, established employees on campus. I hadn't even had a full-time job yet. I suddenly realized that a summer class, offered when most of the student body had gone home, was the best time for campus professionals to further their education.

When the cat's away, the mice come out and move up the corporate ladder.

Our teacher arrived and opened his briefcase. He got straight to the point: we only had one week to do a semester's worth of work. We would start right away, beginning with a project that would culminate in a huge presentation on Friday. To make it more interesting, it would be a competition. The class was split into two teams.

Each team had to come up with a business concept. We had to back that concept up with an airtight proposal and supporting data. It was like we were the pilot project for what would later become the hit TV show *Shark Tank*.

This class had nine sharks and one goldfish. I had no idea what I was doing.

After we split into two teams, we had to select a leader. A make-believe CEO.

You see where this is going, don't you? Yes. They picked me to be CEO.

I don't even remember what the project was. I just remember the overwhelming sense that I was in way over my head. Which was soon replaced by a sense of awe.

I was surrounded by the best team of professionals a CEO could ask for.

The person from the finance office? She was an absolute whiz at crunching numbers. The administrative professional? Rumor had it that she pulled in a gazillion dollars with her grant writing skills. The systems administrator? A computer whiz.

It was easy to assign tasks for this project. Everyone was already an expert at something.

The day of the presentation, my team was up first. I gave a brief introduction and acknowledged everyone's role in the project.

Then I stepped out of the way and let none other than my old PE teacher take the floor. She nailed her part of the presentation. Everyone else followed through as expected.

After both teams had presented their projects, our teacher announced the winner.

"It was really close," he said. "But Mark's team wins."

Whoa!

"Both projects were excellent," our teacher continued. "But did you notice what Mark did from a leadership perspective?"

"Please, no," I thought to myself. "Don't call on me to explain."

I sighed in relief as the teacher kept going and answered his own question.

"He recognized the skills of his teammates," he went on. "He assigned tasks, and then he got out of the way. He let everyone do what they do best. That's one of the most efficient, commonsense ways to lead."

The lesson I learned that day might seem simple at first glance.

Well, duh, just let the pros do what they do best.

But it went further than that. It was a paradigm shift.

In the right context, introverts can be leaders.

The value of introverts as leaders can't be ignored. We live in a society where office politics and cut-throat competition negatively affect so many organizations. There are leaders out there who are more interested in maintaining status quo and holding on to their own power.

Most introverts have no desire for power or attention. An introvert is more likely to do what's in everyone's best interests and then move on, without any need for ego gratification. Our distaste for leadership roles, paradoxically, often makes us more qualified for them.

In other words, we get the job done, and then *poof,* we're outta there.

STEPPING OUT OF YOUR COMFORT ZONE

My first big-time public speaking event was at the Free Library of Philadelphia. Carol Finkle, the founder of Creative Access, arranged the gig. It was part of a city-wide promotion featuring deaf performers, artists, and writers. Carol has always created opportunities for deaf professionals to get noticed.

One problem: as an introvert, I don't want to get noticed.

I'd done presentations at small bookstores and local colleges. I was used to lecturing in front of small groups. The Free Library of Philadelphia was different. They had a huge auditorium that was going to be *packed.* This was the start of my new, ultra-perfectionist work ethic.

There's going to be a couple hundred people there. Let's overprepare, shall we?

The funny thing is that this presentation was about my first book, *Deaf Again.*

What was I overpreparing for? Deaf Again *is an autobiography. You'd think I already knew the material.*

I wrote an outline, compiled notes, rehearsed repeatedly, edited out parts I didn't like, and sharpened the parts I did like. It wasn't long before this presentation was *airtight.* I was now in *The Zone.*

And then came the email.

"Hi Mark," said Carol. "One of the directors at the Free Library would like to treat you to dinner before the event."

Uh-oh.

I tried to politely decline, but there was no way out. The director insisted on showing her gratitude and I didn't want to be rude. There was a nice restaurant right around the corner and it was only a two-minute walk. There was no reasonable excuse to get out of this.

I was stuck. That zone I like to get into before my show? Gone.

Carol and my whole family were treated to a wonderful dinner. I ordered a light meal and went easy on the food. I told Carol that the butterflies in my stomach made me wary of eating too much. She smiled knowingly. She gets me.

An hour later, a special guest stood on the stage in front of a packed auditorium. It was Lorene Cary, who was already an established author. Her job was to introduce me, the green rookie. It was clear from the get-go that she, too, likes to prepare. She began with a heartfelt and impressively accurate summary of my book.

I began to get bad gas.

"And without any further ado..."

My heart pounded. My stomach rumbled. Uh-oh. I think I have to go to the bathroom.

"...the author of *Deaf Again,* Mark Drolsbaugh!"

The bathroom was not an option. I made my way up to the stage. I thanked Lorene and acknowledged the applause. My heart was still pounding. It was showtime.

As I got into the gist of my presentation, I began to relax. It turns out that it does pay to overprepare. The information gets seared into your brain. Once you get on a roll, it starts to flow.

Nice, but I was worried about something else starting to flow. As I paced the stage, I grimaced with the realization that I had the walking farts.

And then I noticed my son Darren in the audience. He was eight years old at the time. He raised his hand and made a comment. It was spot on, and we both shared a laugh. The walking farts were gone. The presentation was a success.

Afterward, I wondered about the mental and gastrointestinal anguish that I had suffered. It clearly wasn't necessary. The audience was fantastic. My family and friends were there. I knew the material like the back of my hand. So why the gastrointestinal fireworks?

Turns out that I'm not the only introvert who goes through these mental gymnastics prior to an event. In *Quiet,* by Susan Cain, there's a chapter that mentions a renowned lecturer by the name of Professor Brian Little. It details his habit of avoiding social interaction before any of his lectures. When his excuse to avoid socialization was taken away from him prior to one of his talks, it threw him off his game.

I could relate. Big time.

Athletes have been known to do whatever they have to do to get into *The Zone* before a big game. Introverts can do the same. Just do the right amount of preparing (or overpreparing, in my case) beforehand. Know your boundaries. Know yourself.

A disclaimer: I have a love-hate relationship with presentations. There are times when I thoroughly enjoy them, and there are times when I say I never want to do this again. Somehow, I wind up doing them again. And I don't want to encourage overpreparing in a bad way. We will examine this in more depth later in the book.

For the most part, I like to stay behind the scenes. But every once in a while, I like to challenge myself to do something out of the ordinary. Just to see if I can. If it's something I'm good at, I don't mind pushing myself a little further. Carol provided such an opportunity and made something wonderful happen. She has opened countless doors for deaf professionals and I'm honored to have been a part of it.

GIVE YOURSELF SOME CREDIT

There's this misconception that *deaf* means *can't hear a thing.* Truth is, deaf people have greatly varying levels of hearing. Some of us can hear low pitches but not high pitches, and for others it's vice versa. Some of us benefit from assistive technology and some of us don't.

Many deaf people, myself included, appreciate music in our own unique way. As a kid, I grew up listening to a wide variety of music. One problem, though.

I could not understand much, if any, of the lyrics to most songs.

AC/DC's *Back in Black* and Aerosmith's *Walk This Way* are examples of kick-ass songs where you can't help but rock to the beat even if you have no idea what the vocalists are saying. Ditto for Queen's *Another One Bites the Dust.*

Then the Internet happened.

Like a kid in a candy shop, I Googled the lyrics for all of my favorite songs.

As mentioned in a previous chapter, I was taken aback. To quote myself:

"The first time I got a glimpse of the lyrics to several rock songs, I was... disappointed. There was a lot of *yeah yeah yeah* and *baby baby baby* with some *I gotta have you so bad* sprinkled in. *That's it? Seriously? There's got to be more to it than this.*"

I had no idea that the lyrics to many songs are inane.

A well a bird, bird, bird, b-bird's the word...

I rest my case.

I'm not saying music is stupid. Some of the craziest lyrics are really catchy and you can't help but sing along.

I'm just saying it was a shock to find out how reality differed from perception.

Seeing how many of the biggest rock acts have performed in front of huge, adoring crowds, I couldn't help but assume that all of them sang some incredibly deep stuff. Some do. Many of them don't. Doesn't matter. If they can carry a tune, it's all good.

The same thing happened with extroverts.

I grew up surrounded by chatty people whose words I could not hear. I assumed they all must be talking about something *deep*.

Turns out that's not true. Hang out with my aunt Emma, and you'll find it's possible to say a lot of nothing for hours on end.

Take it from me: if you're an introvert and you're down on yourself for not being able to carry a conversation like an extrovert... stop. Just because someone is talking doesn't mean that person is the brightest bulb in the chandelier.

In fact, according to research published in *The Leadership Quarterly*, there's something known as the babble hypothesis. It states that people who speak more wind up leading what were initially leaderless groups. Intelligence or personality does not matter. If you talk a lot, you become the de facto leader.

I've seen this happen many times in online breakout sessions. Whoev-

er talks the most becomes the group leader regardless of that person's level of expertise (or lack thereof).

I've thought about this a lot lately. It seems like our politics have arrived at a place where a person who rambles loudly can somehow gain as much (or more) respect as someone who calmly states the facts.

You could jump on the counter at the local supermarket, rant about government oppression, and have a new political party formed before security throws you out.

Just the same as our music, not every leader succeeds on account of pure genius. A lot of leaders get where they are thanks to their extroverted personalities.

Don't sell yourself short. You have the same, if not better, qualities of any leader out there. You're creative and most likely a deliberate thinker. Sounds pretty qualified to me.

Not buying it? Okay, then. How about this quote from Plato:

Only those who do not seek power are qualified to hold it.

It's true. Too many times, the people most qualified to be leaders don't want to be leaders. Especially introverts. It's a moral dilemma. We're ridiculously talented, but leadership roles make us ridiculously uncomfortable.

There are some introverted leaders who are blessed because they can genuinely lead without sacrificing who they are. They can lead from behind the shadows. Or maybe they have the right balance between working with others and having ample recharge time.

There's a fine line. Introvert leaders are often at risk for burnout because the predominantly extroverted (and therefore overstimulating) office environment exhausts them.

Leadership roles may or may not be for you (for me, they're not).

But never doubt your talents. Never doubt that you do have a lot to offer, one way or the other. Never sell yourself short.

And don't forget the bird's the word.

DON'T POP THE BUBBLE

There's a question people ask that sets off an uncontrolled chain reaction in my mind.

"So, Mark, are you working on another book?"

I blanch. And then I trip all over myself trying to come up with a coherent answer.

Words escape me.

"Uh, ah, actually, yeah, there's this thing, kinda sorta, I'm a bit busy, but yeah, I hope to be kind of working on something, uh, something a bit different, eventually."

What the hell did I just say?

"So you *are* writing a book?"

"Uh..."

Slowly, I gather my wits. And still say something vague.

"I'm always writing," I reply.

And then *poof,* I'm outta there.

What just happened?

I've always attributed this to superstition.

I'm a baseball lifer. Baseball players are superstitious. If we go on a hot hitting streak, we might wear the same underwear for days on end.

Without washing said underwear. We don't want to wash the good mojo out of it.

There's another superstition that has long been part of baseball's unwritten rules:

If the pitcher is throwing a no-hitter, for chrissakes, don't say anything. Otherwise you'll jinx it.

This kind of superstition has been validated by statistics geeks on television. It happens all the time.

It's the bottom of the ninth. Our top relief pitcher is on the mound. He strikes out the first two hitters. Only one more out and we wrap the game up.

And then the caption appears:

BRAD McNULTY HAS NOT GIVEN UP A HOME RUN IN 47 INNINGS.

Crack!

Aw, shit.

It happens in basketball, too.

THE KNICKS HAVE NOT SCORED A BASKET IN 4:42.

Swish!

Moral of the story: if you got something good going on, *shut up.*

One thing I never did as a baseball player was chew tobacco. But I did stuff my mouth with bubble gum. I developed an affinity for something called Hubba Bubba. It must have been derived from Krazy Glue. You could blow the biggest bubbles with that stuff.

Unless your friends were watching.

I'd get this good chew going, take a deep breath, and then slowly but surely, have this pink monstrosity growing out of my mouth. It would reach *Guinness World Records* proportions and then—

Whap!

Never blow a world record bubble anywhere in the vicinity of your teammates.

For similar reasons, I apply this to my writing endeavors. I say nothing as much as possible when working on a project.

And when asked if I'm working on a project, I regurgitate nonsensical words.

I have this internalized belief that when I'm writing a blog, an article, or a book, it's like blowing a bubble. It needs to develop slowly and surely at its own pace. Without any intrusion from anyone who may pop it.

This is where introversion, not superstition, comes into play.

Introverts thrive on accomplishment. In an introverted manner, of course.

We like to get lost in our thoughts. We love getting ideas and inspiration, and then acting on them. Good things happen. We enjoy the results.

But we don't necessarily enjoy the attention that comes with the results.

Or, even worse, *before* the results.

I love writing books. I'm happy to share them with the world after they're done.

But if people find out about a book before I finish it, we're going to have introvert problems.

If I tell other people what I'm doing before I'm done doing what I'm doing, two things usually happen. Neither of them good.

One, people start asking questions.

What are you writing about? When is it coming out?

This leads to conversations I'm not comfortable having. I'm already stressing over the weight of my own high expectations without dragging other people into it.

Some people like to announce their goals to the world because it creates a sense of accountability. It pushes them to get stuff done. If you're a procrastinator, this is actually a good approach. Go ahead, give yourself a public kick in the butt. But for most introverts, we've already set the bar high. We don't need to add any external motivators. It's our internal world that drives us.

Two, a lot of people like to offer advice.

Why are you writing about this, but not that? I suggest you add more of that.

And the worst one of them all:

I want to talk to you about your book.

Just to be clear: I don't mind talking about my books *after* they've been published. But when someone wants to discuss a book while it's still in progress, it derails my train of thought.

Introverts don't want this kind of attention, especially if we're people pleasers. We may wind up trying to appease everyone else's ideas and suggestions, only to later realize that what we originally wanted to say just went off the rails.

There's another factor in play: we really don't handle interruptions that well. Especially if they interrupt our train of thought. Jenn Granneman, in an article titled *These 19 'Extroverted' Behaviors Annoy Introverts the Most,* said it best:

"...introverts tend to focus deeply, so when they're suddenly forced to shift their attention elsewhere, it can be like trying to swim back to shore in a lake made of peanut butter."

The best solution for this? Say nothing. Work in solitude. It's your area of strength.

There's a reason some of my colleagues have literally hid me in a basement office when a time-sensitive report needed to be done. They've noticed that I work more efficiently when I'm allowed to hear my own thoughts without interruption.

And then, when your goals are met—be it a new book, a new job, a promotion—announce it after the fact. Surprise everyone. One day you're quietly going about your business, and then the next day you've floored someone with an unexpected accomplishment.

It has more impact when you've blown everyone away out of the blue. You've exceeded everyone's expectations *because they never had any expectations to begin with.* You pulled the rug out from under them, and now they want to know how you did it.

There is such a thing as an Introvert Aura. Make it work for you.

Shock the world.

And then *poof,* you're outta there.

Your work is done.

.

THAT WAS AWKWARD

A s I walked past Melanie in our home office, I notice she appeared to be watching an episode of *The Brady Bunch* on her computer. I raised my drink and said a quick hello.

Whoops. That wasn't the Brady Bunch. It was Melanie's online American Sign Language class.

"Whoa!" I exclaimed, jumping out of the webcam's line of sight. "My bad."

"Oh, it's fine," Melanie smiled. "Would you like to say hello to my class?"

"Uhhhh," I stammered. A sense of dread enveloped me. It was a familiar sense of dread. I couldn't remember when or where I felt it before, but it was definitely familiar.

I discretely pantomimed 47 different versions of the word "no."

"Oh, come on," Melanie insisted. "They'd love to meet you. Really, it's fine."

"It's not fine," I thought to myself. "I always make an ass out of myself in situations like this."

At this point Melanie noticed I wasn't comfortable. She offered me an out.

"You don't have to if you're busy," she said. "But a quick hello would be great."

My overthinking, highly sensitive introvert brain was now in overdrive. I couldn't say no because Melanie asked me in front of her students. They knew I was there. I didn't want to disappoint them.

The reason for my reluctance? I'm terrible when called on to say something on a moment's notice. I always wind up putting my foot in my mouth.

Suck it up, Drolz. If you make an ass out of yourself, you make an ass out of yourself. So be it.

I knelt down next to Melanie's chair so that I was in full view of the webcam.

"Hi," I greeted the class. They smiled and waved back.

So far, so good.

"Nice to meet you," I continued. "Are you looking forward to summer vac—"

"Wait, hold up," Melanie cautioned. "This is my ASL 1 class. Slow down a bit."

Oops.

"ASL 1?" I asked. "I'm surprised. You're doing great. I didn't know you were beginners."

More smiles.

Nice recovery, Drolz.

We did a brief introduction. I noticed some of the students did a double take when they saw my name sign. Melanie was already on top of it.

"Could you explain to them how you got your name sign?"

"Sure," I replied. "It happened when I was on the Gallaudet baseball team and—"

"Slow down, slow down," Melanie reminded me.

Once again, I was signing at full speed in front of a beginner's ASL class. It's my natural tendency to speed up whenever I feel awkward.

"Oops, sorry," I smiled. "Okay, let's start again. My name sign is Drool. In a professional setting I prefer fingerspelling M-A-R-K, but my friends call me Drool."

Blank stares.

Here we go. The part where the Drolz Train goes off the rails.

"Why do they call you Drool?" Melanie asked, trying to guide this train wreck of a conversation somewhere positive.

"I have no idea," I replied, nonchalantly taking a sip from my drink and drooling it all over my shirt.

One student laughed. He got the joke. The rest of them continued to stare. Only now it was more of a wide-eyed stare.

"But seriously," Melanie prodded. "Tell them what happened."

"It's a nickname that was given to me in college," I went on. "It's not really D-R-O-O-L. It's D-R-O-L-Z. Some people on the baseball team had trouble spelling my last name. My baseball coach tried to help them out. He said it's D-R-O-L... you know, almost like drool... S-B-A-U-G-H. Next thing you know, Drool became my name sign. You sign Drool, but my nickname is actually Drolz."

The blank stares gradually morphed into smiles.

Nice recovery again. I think.

"I know it looks weird to the casual observer," I acknowledged. "Which is why I prefer to just fingerspell M-A-R-K in a professional setting. The name sign is more like a nickname used by those who know me well."

Some students wondered: *if the name sign is so goofy, why not change it?* Melanie pointed out that this is next to impossible. In the deaf community, she explained, a name sign is not something you make up on a whim. It's given to you by others based on something unique about you. And then it sticks.

I chimed in with another anecdote. I told the class that when I moved back to Philadelphia from Washington D.C., I tried to leave my name sign behind. Didn't work. It followed me. All it took was one friend from D.C. who visited Philly and next thing you know, the entire Philly deaf community called me Drool. Thirty years later, they still do.

"A name sign is like a tattoo," I added. "Once you get one, you can't get rid of it."

Almost immediately after saying that, I noticed one of the students had tattoos all over her arms. She didn't seem amused.

Foot, meet mouth.

Later that evening, I checked in with Melanie.

"I didn't offend your student, did I?" I asked.

"Huh? What do you mean?"

"I said name signs are like tattoos. Then I noticed one of your students has a ton of them. I don't think that went over well."

"Oh, she's good. They all enjoyed meeting you."

"Okay, great. Sometimes I get caught off guard when we do something spontaneous. It's like those icebreakers at work. I always mess those up."

Hey! That sense of dread that seemed so familiar? I suddenly remembered what it was. Icebreakers. They suck.

There's a blog called *Introvert, Dear* by Jenn Granneman. It's powerful and features many contributing writers. If you're an introvert, check it out. You'll immediately feel like you belong.

Which is exactly what happened when I went there and read an article that explained why I trip all over myself during icebreakers.

It was an article by Monique Hebert titled *Dear Workplaces, Churches, and Schools, PLEASE Stop Doing Icebreakers. Signed, Introverts.* Hebert knocked it out of the park. She made the connection between introverts' tendency to rely on long-term memory and our struggle to come up with something on the fly.

It takes longer for introverts to gather our thoughts. A spontaneous activity such as an icebreaker, especially without any advance warning, is a recipe for disaster. An activity that's supposed to help people bond may actually cause stress.

I need an answer to an off-the-point question someone asked me out of the blue and I need it now! Shit, I don't have it! Abandon ship!

Icebreakers are perpetually awkward. As Hebert explains it, whenever it's our turn to talk during an icebreaker, chaos ensues. The words simply don't come out the way we want them to. We trip all over ourselves. Next thing you know, an activity that was meant to loosen us up has the opposite effect. Our anxiety goes through the roof.

In the next chapter, you'll see that it's possible to develop improvisation skills. If this is something you'd like to do, and if you're comfortable with it, that's fine. But should you be *required* to do it? No. Should you suck it up and allow your employer (or, ahem, your significant other) to put you on the spot? No. Especially if it makes you uncomfortable.

Communicate. That's all you really need to do. I've told my colleagues that if they plan another impromptu icebreaker without any advance notice, I'm taking an impromptu bathroom break.

Tell your employer, your friends, and your partners that you function much better when they give you a heads-up. Then you can draw upon the very long-term memory that's a *strength* for you. Not only can you make it work for you, it benefits them, too. It assures them they'll get the best you have to offer.

That's right. Reframe this. Not being able to answer a question immediately is not a weakness. It's just your mind operating differently. An Olympic gold medal sprinter and an Olympic gold medal marathoner are both gold medalists. They just work at a different pace. Nothing wrong with that.

(OMEDY (ENTRAL

I've been told it's good to get out of your comfort zone. It adds a little excitement to your life. Sometimes I go along with that advice. Sometimes I regret it. This was one of those times.

I was barely through the first five minutes of my *Madness in the Mainstream* presentation when the realization hit me:

I'm bombing. Badly.

At the beginning of this book, I mentioned my fear of public speaking. This particular presentation was Exhibit A on why I feel that way.

There were 150 people. All of them looking back at me with blank stares.

I was going nowhere fast.

I decided to get there faster.

I sped up my presentation. I rushed through the next few slides.

More blank stares.

This was new territory for me. Most of my presentations are for audiences that are already in my corner (such as the deaf community, ASL students, educators who support the use of sign language in the classroom, and parents who are aware of all of the above). The things I say validate what they knew all along. I offer them solutions for problems they already want to solve.

Sometimes I go in front of audiences that are *against* me. Usually this involves educators, administrators, and legislators who oppose sign language for whatever reason. I actually get a kick out of this. I can see the defensive posturing at the beginning, the slow but steady increase of smiles as I begin to win them over, and an eventual *"a-ha. I get what you're saying."*

A crowd that's for or against you has energy. You can feed off that energy.

But a crowd with nothing but blank stares? It's a public speaker's worst nightmare. Amplified a thousand-fold for the introvert.

Get me out of here!

I was actually sweating. Once that first drip of sweat works its way down your brow, you're screwed. Telling yourself to stop sweating only opens the floodgates. It felt like my suit was a portable sauna.

Finally, someone threw me a lifeline. It was Stephanie, my anchor in the crowd. She caught my attention with a discreet wave.

"Drolz!" Stephanie mouthed. "Slow down. Breathe. Take your time."

Stephanie held her hands up and slowly lowered them onto her desk, hypnotically guiding me into a calmer state of mind.

The train was back on track.

I took a deep breath and surveyed the room. Then I pulled myself together.

"What's different about this crowd?" I asked myself.

They were all parents of deaf children. I had done successful presentations with parents before, but this group was really new. Everything I had said so far was in stark contrast with what medical professionals had recently told them. They were shell-shocked.

"This is a lot to digest, isn't it?" I asked. Some of the people in the audience nodded.

"I know. There's nothing more maddening than being a parent of a deaf kid and having a ton of experts giving you conflicting information. It's okay. You *will* reach a place where you can sort this out and do what's best for your children."

I could feel the room relax. Or maybe it was just me. Either way, all was good.

"I wish I could say everything will get better *right now*. It won't. You're going to see a lot of irrational stuff out there. But you *will* know it when you see it, and you *will* be the best advocates your kids could ever ask for. For example..."

I went on my infamous Diversity Day Rant.

"My deaf son went to a mainstream school that celebrates Diversity Day. Don't get me wrong, I'm all for it. But they missed the bus with the deaf kids. It's absurd. They literally *separate deaf kids from each other* because of different communication styles and assistive technology. My son was not allowed to interact with another deaf kid in his school because that kid was not allowed to use sign language. They were afraid my son's sign language would interfere with the other kid's auditory-verbal therapy. Which is ridiculous, because nothing empowers a deaf kid more than seeing other deaf kids succeeding in different ways. They learn from, and support each other, in ways that no one else can."

I was just getting warmed up.

"It was Diversity Day at my son's school, and they made a big celebration out of it. Celebrate this, celebrate that. Let's all get together and sing Kumba—HEY! Keep those deaf kids apart! You might cross-contaminate them or something!"

The crowd loosened up. They laughed along with the rant while nodding along with the important message behind it.

You know who my inspiration was for that rant?

George Carlin.

"This is a country where tobacco kills four hundred thousand people a year, so they ban artificial sweeteners... because a rat died!"

The late, great George Carlin has had a powerful influence on me. I've watched so many of his shows that I've internalized the way he gets his message across. Anytime I go on a rant, like the one in front of those parents, my Inner George is released.

Humor can get you through the toughest challenges. I always enjoy losing myself in a big serving of laughs. Doesn't matter what kind. I'm a sucker for stand-up, movies, sitcoms, or idiotic shows such as truTV's *Impractical Jokers*.

Over the years, I've developed a deeper appreciation of stand-up comedy. It's an art form. Every comedian has their own style and delivery. One might have you in stitches for an entire set. Another might only make you laugh once every five minutes, but still hold you in rapt attention for a full hour.

If you get into the habit of watching comedy all the time, you absorb it. It comes in handy. You develop your improvisational skills and it can get you out of an awkward mess. Just like my aforementioned presentation that went downhill fast.

Believe it or not, improv is a skill that can be developed. My friends and I are huge fans of the wildly popular Whose Line Is It Anyway? *television show, and we've created our own version at parties. We've noticed that the more you play, the better you get at it.*

Watch the comics. They're master storytellers. Their posture, their delivery, and their timing are amazing. It's something all of them have worked on and perfected through years of hard work. If you watch closely enough, you can wire your brain for it. You can channel it whenever you need it.

This is something that's hard to explain because it seems contradictory. Many introverts, including me, struggle to find the right words on a moment's notice. This is why I'm uncomfortable at job interviews and Q&A sessions. But when it comes to having a sense of humor, somehow

I can use that to get out of a tight spot. Noted author and entrepreneur James Altucher, who is also an introvert, has encouraged people to develop their idea muscle. In a similar vein, I believe it's possible to develop a comedy muscle.

A few years after Stephanie bailed me out, there was another presentation that went completely off the rails. It was a large crowd and I had gone so far off the point, I couldn't remember what I was trying to say. There was only one thing to do.

Panic!

This time around, there wasn't anyone to save me from myself. But there was one other thing I could do, other than panic.

Roll with it. Be in the moment and share it with your audience.

"How about that?" I said. "I have no idea where I'm going with this. Let's back up a bit and figure out what the hell I was saying."

The audience laughed. I relaxed.

Sometimes, when there's an elephant in the room, the best way to defuse the tension is to pet the elephant.

Embracing an awkward moment helps you conquer it. By rolling with it instead of trying to fix it, it fixes itself.

MENTAL GYMNASTICS

A t times in this book I've encouraged overpreparing as a means of eliminating anxiety.

Nervous about a presentation? Practice it until you know it like the back of your hand.

It's just like in sports. If you methodically prepare for game situations in practice, during the actual game your skills will naturally take over. Athletes often refer to this as being in *The Zone*. With the right amount of practice and talent, you reach a level of expertise that's described in the psychology field as *unconscious competence.*

The same thing applies to music. Did Jimi Hendrix ever think about what notes he had to play when he jammed on stage? He didn't. He just grabbed his guitar and, with who knows how many hours of practice behind him, let it fly.

That said, know the difference between meticulous preparation and overthinking. One enhances your skills and helps you find The

Zone. The other drives you up the wall. There comes a time when you have to go *"shush!"* and quiet your mind.

News Flash: some introverts also have anxiety.

One of the most powerful presentations I've ever attended was given by Dr. Sam Trychin. He wasn't talking about introverts, but he might as well have been.

At this particular presentation, Dr. Trychin—who is hard of hearing—addressed issues that hard of hearing people have to deal with.

Dr. Trychin stated that many hard of hearing people tend to assume all of the responsibility for communication. It's a burden they put on themselves.

Speaking from personal experience, I can vouch that it's not just the hard of hearing. There are plenty of deaf people who do the same.

Communication is a two-way street. But because deaf and hard of hearing people are in the minority, we sometimes get into the habit of perceiving any communication breakdown as something that's entirely our fault.

Here's a paradigm shift: every now and then, a store clerk rolls his eyes when I say "pardon me, I'm deaf." It's as if I'm apologizing for who I am. But when I respond to a question I didn't understand by asking for clarification in American Sign Language, it gets a different response. The clerk makes the effort to use visual gestural communication or writes on a notepad. When I respect myself, the clerk respects me, too.

Dr. Trychin took this another step further. When we assume all of the responsibility for communication, he explained, there are significant consequences. Not only are we mentally exhausted, but we trigger physical symptoms, as well. Among the symptoms are muscle tension, back pain, neck pain, high blood pressure, anxiety, irritability, stomach pain, and more.

Waitaminute. Did he say anxiety?

While writing this chapter, I did some extra research and found another introvert who wrote *exactly* what Dr. Trychin said, except it was the introvert version. Jenn Granneman, author of *The Secret*

Lives of Introverts: Inside our Hidden World, has an article titled *15 Signs You're an Introvert With High-Functioning Anxiety*. It's posted in *Introvert, Dear*, her award-winning online community.

That's when it hit me. Not only are we introverts, but some of us, myself included, have anxiety issues. If you're an introvert, you can probably relate.

Why? Because we live in this internal world where sometimes, our thoughts are so powerful, they take on an energy of their own. It's like water. Sometimes water is calm, soothing, meditative, and refreshing. In a monsoon, not so much. Our thoughts can likewise go either way. One moment we're blissfully lost in our own thoughts, and then in another moment our minds are spinning with anxiety-inducing, worst-case scenarios.

It was in the calm, soothing, meditative environment of my own mind where I came up with the material for my first book, *Deaf Again*. By letting my mind flow, it effortlessly created chapter after chapter. It's a book that gives a rare inside look of what it feels like to be deaf.

"This book is going to be the mother lode of deaf literature," I thought to myself.

And then I let my mind go off to the races.

"What if this book upsets or offends people in my family? I have so many relatives who meant well, but they're not deaf. They just didn't understand. This book explains how and why. Oh my god. They're going to be pissed. Let me clean this up a little."

I actually went through a mental inventory of everyone in my family who might be upset. I imagined all of the possible reactions of anyone who might be offended. I mentally prepared a dissertation-level defense for each and every one of them. I sweated out every little detail.

Oh, and I wasn't done there.

My mind was no longer off to the races. It was off the rails.

Once I convinced myself I wouldn't be disowned by my family, I relaxed. For maybe a minute. Then I thought *waitaminute*. What about my friends? My colleagues? My supervisor? My supervisor's supervisor? The President of the United States?

Wash, rinse, repeat.

The thought never occurred to me to just trust the process, to let the chips fall where they may, and to respond to any challenges only if it was worthwhile to do so.

In most cases, it's not. We can't make everyone happy, can we?

Eventually we learn that we can do whatever we want without worrying what others think. Part of this awakening comes from maturity.

Around the time I hit 50, I gradually started losing my ability to worry about what others might think. I wish I had learned this much earlier. It's so liberating. You realize you don't have to be perfect and no one will bite you when you're not. You let go.

Like in this paragraph, for example. I'm a meticulous editor who has been described as anal retentive by other writers. But look at me now. Other editters are probbly banging they're heds on there desks. I don't care. How refreshing is that?

As introverts, we live in our own world where our thoughts go so deep, sometimes we disconnect from everyone else. It's a fully inward, total retreat. It's actually a nice place to be. If you're absorbed in your own thoughts, enjoy them. Just be sure you know the difference between *enjoying your inner world* and *ruminating over things we have no control over.*

There have been times—especially at the office—when I've said nothing at all not because I couldn't find the words, but because my mind was too busy overanalyzing every little detail. It's like that scene in *Avengers: Infinity War* when Dr. Strange tuned out everything going on around him. When asked what he was doing, he replied that he had analyzed 14,000,605 different possible outcomes.

I can relate.

For me, the best way to deal with overthinking is to catch myself in the act. A little *oops I did it again* helps me put the brakes on a spiraling mind. Sometimes, someone else catches me in the act. In which case I immediately acknowledge what's going on.

"Drolz? Hello? Are you even paying attention?"

"I'm fine," I reply, with a deadpan expression. *"I'm mentally processing 14,000,605 different possible outcomes."*

And then I relax.

PART III
INTROVERTS AT WORK

SUPER INTROVERT

It was my first day on the job as a supermarket stock clerk. I was only 17 years old at the time, and it felt like I was wandering the halls of Berkshire Hathaway. I was assigned to work in the general merchandise department. I grinned nervously as my new boss, Jerry, led me on a tour of the premises.

As we made our way through the store, Jerry introduced me to as many coworkers as he could. We went through dairy, produce, frozen foods, customer service, the deli, and the front office. Jerry was clearly an outgoing person who was easy to get along with. Everyone he introduced me to seemed to share similar outgoing traits.

Then we went to the back room of the general merchandise department. The team was there on a quick break. Except for one. I couldn't help but notice one solitary worker still on the floor, stocking the shelves with toothpaste.

"Who's that?" I asked.

"Oh, that's Howard," Jerry replied, with a brief sigh. We walked over to say hello.

"Hey, Howard," Jerry waved. Howard didn't respond. He seemed fully immersed in his own world of toothpaste.

"Howard?" Jerry repeated.

"Oh, hello!" Howard looked up, completely caught off guard.

"This is the new guy. Howard, Mark. Mark, Howard."

Howard smiled as we shook hands. He seemed nice enough. But I got the sense that Jerry didn't have the same opinion.

My hunch proved correct. After we returned to the back room, Jerry gave me a little heads-up.

"Just so you know," Jerry cautioned. "Howard's actually a nice guy. But he's not a team player. If you want to learn anything, hang out with me and Ron. We'll show you the ropes."

Ron walked up and shook my hand.

"Yeah," Ron added. "Let me know if you need anything. For now, all you need is this." He directed my attention to the coffee machine.

"Or maybe this." He pointed to a stack of magazines on the desk.

They were raunchy magazines.

Jerry and Ron burst out laughing.

"We rotate working the weekend night shift," Jerry continued.

"And that'll keep you awake," Ron laughed. "But seriously. The night shift is tough. Make as much coffee as you want."

Jerry and Ron left. I grabbed a cart stacked with boxes of deodorant to wheel out and unpack. I sensed someone behind me.

It was Howard. He was done with the toothpaste and came back for mouthwash.

"Your first day on the job," he smiled. "And they're teaching you how to get zonked out on caffeine and smut." He shook his head as he wheeled the mouthwash out.

I like this guy.

As I stocked the shelves with deodorant, I was right down the aisle from where Howard worked on a mouthwash promotional display. I couldn't help but notice his reaction when an announcement blared over the speakers.

"General merchandise department, report to the conference room at 10:45 sharp."

Howard's shoulders slumped. He looked up at the ceiling and eye-rolled.

"It's the Grand Poobah," he sighed.

"Who's the Grand Poobah?" I asked.

"That's Jim. The general manager. He likes to hear himself talk. He thinks he inspires us to work. But he might like to, you know, actually let us work."

Howard was genuinely annoyed with the impromptu meeting. I also noticed he had gone through boxes of mouthwash much faster than the average stock clerk. He was almost done with what was an elaborate display. And now he had to stop, just short of finishing his task, to listen to someone talk about how to finish tasks.

"Look," Howard explained. "When Poobah talks, you listen. Just smile and nod your head. He likes that."

"I can do that."

"Great. But whatever you do... do *not* ask him a question. He'll go on for another 30 minutes. Just smile, nod, and we're outta there."

Now I really like this guy.

A few weeks later, Howard was slated to go on vacation. I was assigned to cover his duties while he was out.

I was in the main back room where a group of employees from all departments often had lunch together. Except for Howard. He always ate alone in the general merchandise back room. It seemed to rub other employees the wrong way. It may have given them the impression that he thought he was too good for them.

He didn't. I didn't understand it at the time, but this highly likeable yet seemingly antisocial guy was simply recharging. On his own, like all introverts do.

"Hey Mark?" said Jerry, right before lunch break was over. "Make sure you check with Howard before he goes on vacation. He'll help you pick up where he left off."

"Got it," I confirmed. "Where is he?"

"Probably in our back room," Jerry shrugged.

"With a magazine," Ron added. Ron pantomimed flipping a magazine open and gawking at the centerfold. The room erupted in laughter. I shook my head and left.

I found Howard in the general merchandise back room.

He was alone.

With a magazine.

"Howard?"

He looked up. I caught the cover of the magazine.

Investor's Business Daily.

I chuckled at the irony of it all. The alpha males were together in a large back room where they talked sports, cars, and trashy magazines. Howard was by himself, researching the stock market.

Howard put the magazine down and we did a quick run-through of his inventory. He had his own style of ordering merchandise. I was impressed. He had this analytic way of observing people and then placing orders based on their behavior. We had our own data that did the same thing, but Howard was ahead of it. He identified trends before the computer did. Sometimes this got him in trouble as he didn't always conform with company guidelines.

This quiet dude may have been perceived as a rebel, but he was also a genius.

While we did the inventory check, I also noticed that Howard always greeted individual customers with a kind, welcoming demeanor.

He avoided large groups, but was attentive to individuals. Sound familiar?

One of the customers was a regular. An older man who shopped in the store on a daily basis. Howard filled me in on the guy's story.

"That's Vinnie. He comes in and buys the same thing every day. One orange. One banana. A newspaper and a pack of cigarettes."

Sure enough, that's what Vinnie did. It took him at least an hour to gather those four items. He always stopped to chat with any of the store employees who were willing to give him a moment of their time. Howard was one of them.

Vinnie didn't have any family. We were his family.

At the end of our shift, Howard and I punched out and headed to the parking lot together. A woman I had never seen before ran up and gave him a bear hug.

"Have a wonderful vacation, Howard!" she gushed. "Mwah! You earned it!" She waved goodbye and scampered into the store.

"That's Louise," he laughed. "She'll flirt you up, but she's harmless. She lost her husband five years ago. She's been through a lot."

By this point Howard had evolved from reclusive supermarket clerk to Buddha, Jesus, and Gandhi all wrapped up in one.

"Have a great vacation," I said.

"Thank you," Howard replied, as he hopped into his Volkswagen Rabbit.

Major double take.

Howard didn't care that he was driving a car so small, he could park it inside the store if he wanted to. This was during a time when a lot of guys drove a Mustang, a Firebird, or a Camaro. Howard had no interest in a vehicle that would draw that kind of attention.

"Hey," he said, noticing my look of surprise. "This thing gets great mileage. I take it to the shore every weekend."

Say what?

Yes, every weekend. Howard has a house at the Jersey Shore. He doesn't rent it. He *owns* it. He has a boat, too. Apparently, he spends and invests wisely. Only a few people know this.

There's nothing glamorous about Howard's lifestyle. He keeps to himself. And yet he has two homes, two cars (there's another one he shares with his family), a boat, and a beautiful sunset he can watch any evening.

If I had known I was going to write this book 35 years after the fact, I would have followed Howard around and taken notes.

Being around Howard is a lesson in humility and success. He's like a hero of sorts.

It's a bird! It's a plane! No, wait. I have no idea. He's still in the house. He hasn't come out yet. Oh. It's Super Introvert!

Looking back, I realize I was blessed to work with the world's best-kept secret.

JOB INTERVIEWS FOR INTROVERTS

The interview started off innocently enough.

"Tell me what you would bring to this job."

"I'm working toward a degree in psychology and will eventually become a counselor. This is a great place to start."

Score!

It was the winter of 1988 and I was interviewing for a position as Resident Advisor at the Pennsylvania School for the Deaf. I was a mere 22 years old at the time.

This would be my first genuinely challenging job. By *challenging*, I mean *actually working with people*. Up until that point I'd worked as a pool cleaner, a dishwasher, and a supermarket stock clerk. I pretty much minded my own business at each of those jobs. Other than the occasional interruption or supervisory feedback, I lived in my own world. I did whatever I had to do in meditative peace. Other employees often had a radio blaring somewhere, but not me. I was blissfully lost in my own thoughts.

It was a great place to be. My mind was perpetually tuned in to the Drolz Channel. Nothing else mattered.

And then someone from out of nowhere had the audacity to pull me out of my little paradise at the supermarket. It was Linda Baine, the Coordinator of Residence Education at PSD. She was on a mission to recruit me for a job opening.

"Recruit" is an understatement. She stalked me.

A previous Resident Advisor had resigned, and Linda saw me as the perfect replacement. She approached me at my job. Repeatedly. By her third visit, she finally convinced me to get out of my comfort zone at the supermarket and consent to an interview at PSD.

Soon I found myself in the office of Assistant Head of School Dom Bonura, answering what I thought would be softball questions.

"Would you be able to balance this job with your studies?" Dom inquired.

"Absolutely," I replied. "All of my classes are in the morning. I can easily make it here for the second shift."

Piece of cake. Just give me the keys and I'll start next week.

"Okay," Dom continued. "Now tell me... what would you do if a student threw a chair at you?"

Say what?

Seeing how Linda had actively recruited me, I thought the job was already mine. But Dom wasn't playing softball. He threw a high and tight fastball that I wasn't prepared for. There were actually some students with behavioral issues, and he wanted to know how I would handle a difficult situation.

"Excuse me?" I asked, buying myself a little time.

I had nothing. I mentally kicked myself for not being prepared.

"What would you do if a student threw a chair at you?" Dom repeated.

"Throw it back," I nonchalantly replied.

Did I really say that? What was wrong with me? It was the only answer I could come up with. And it was a total non-answer.

Dom stared at me for what felt like an eternity.

And then he burst out laughing. He shifted in his seat and looked at Linda.

"This guy has a sense of humor," he chuckled. He thanked me and said he would get back to me soon.

I got the job. Linda later told me that my brain fart had worked in my favor. Apparently, Dom thought the students would benefit from having a deaf role model with a sense of humor. I lucked out.

Lucky or not, I learned a valuable lesson. *Always be prepared for an interview.* This is a universal truth for anyone, but it carries a lot more weight for introverts.

That brain fart I had? It's nothing new for introverts. We take longer to process our thoughts. In a job interview, which is both stressful and time-sensitive, we're at risk of drawing a total blank. Which I did, save for a lucky off-the-cuff joke that got me the job.

Later that evening, right before bedtime, my mind drifted back to the question that stumped me. Of course, *now* I had all the answers. I thought of several strategies that would have worked in the hypothetical chair-throwing scenario. Every strategy I came up with was consistent with what I had learned in a childhood and adolescent psychology class a few years ago. My answers were spot on. It's just that they popped up in my head at 11:00pm, long after the interview had ended.

The answers were always there. They just happened to be stored away in my long-term memory, as is often the case with introverts.

If you're an introvert and you have a job interview coming up, the best thing to do is go into full Chris Rock mode. Research. Prepare. Rehearse. Overprepare.

Yes, I'm encouraging you to be obsessive-compulsive. But it pays off.

Study the company where you're applying for a job. Be prepared to show your knowledge of said company. This means not only being prepared to answer questions, but being prepared to ask your own questions.

"I noticed your state-of-the-art Information Technology department. Is there a way I can collaborate with them to offer our students accessible technology during evening study hours?"

Be prepared to toot your own horn. This is another thing introverts don't like to do. We don't like to draw attention to ourselves, and talking about our accomplishments does exactly that. But a job interview is no place to be modest. If talking about yourself makes you uncomfortable, do so in a way that shows how your talents benefit others. This will deflect some of the attention off of you and onto the people you will work with.

"I also have an associate's degree in graphic design. I would love to work with the yearbook committee in the afterschool program."

Research, prepare, rehearse, overprepare. Wash, rinse, repeat. And then you'll be ready to duck any chair thrown your way.

SHOCK THE WORLD

Jim Henderson, a self-described "big-time introvert," landed a job in public relations for a computer technology firm in New Jersey. Unfortunately for Jim, *public relations* has *extrovert* written all over it.

For the first couple of years, Jim worked outside of his comfort zone. His considerable knowledge and expertise allowed him to do well. But no matter how successful he was, he was always in a constant state of near-exhaustion. He was stuck in a revolving door where his energy was repeatedly drained and recharged, day in and day out.

And then Jim caught a lucky break. There was an opening in research and development. He successfully applied for the new job. He was now in his element.

A quiet little cubicle. A computer. Tons of data. Minimal interaction with others. For Jim, this was paradise.

In his new role, Jim still collaborated with public relations. But he no longer had to work extensively with the public relations team, go on road trips, or make sales pitches. He would compile the research and data he had, write website content, and assist with the creation of presentation materials that he himself would never have to present. Sure, every now and then some guy in public relations got all the credit for presentations that were driven by Jim's research, but Jim didn't mind. In fact, he liked it that way.

And then there was a huge national conference. Attendance mandatory for all, even Jim. Jim reluctantly packed his bags and flew cross country to Silicon Valley. He arrived at the conference, checked in, and went straight to his room. He ordered room service, caught up with the news on TV, and went over some presentation materials he had prepared for a colleague.

Meanwhile, several reps from his company were still in the hotel lobby, schmoozing and networking. Jim didn't care. All that mattered was getting the presentation materials ready for that evening's workshop.

Jim double checked his files and all looked good. Sighing contentedly, he kicked off his shoes and hopped into bed for a power nap.

The phone rang.

"Jim? It's Eddie. Where the hell are you?"

"Upstairs. Just going over my notes."

"You're missing happy hour. You might want a drink when you get a load of *this*."

Jim sighed. Whatever *this* was, it reinforced his aversion to picking up the phone.

"What happened?"

"Nick missed his connecting flight. The next one is tomorrow morning."

"But... his presentation is tonight."

"Yeah. About that. You're the only one who knows his material.

Shit, you *wrote* his material. We're going to need you tonight."

"You've gotta be kidding me, Eddie."

"Do I sound like I'm kidding?"

"Shit. What about Mike?"

"He's not due to present until tomorrow night. So he's at the bar and... he's hammered."

"I'll meet you downstairs in an hour," Jim sighed.

After a quick strategic meeting, Eddie and Jim set up the conference room with all of the materials and technology that Nick was supposed to use. Only now, it was Jim's show. Jim took a deep breath as conference attendees filed in and took their seats. The room was packed to capacity.

Mike plopped in the seat next to Eddie in the back row, still buzzed from one too many Appletinis.

"Say..." Mike slurred. "What's Jim doing up there?"

"Nick missed his flight," Eddie replied. "Jim's covering for him."

"You've gotta be kidding me, Eddie."

"That's exactly what Jim said."

"This is like *Revenge of the Nerds*. You just put Booger in charge."

"Nah. Trust me. Jim got this."

The master of ceremonies introduced Jim. Jim confidently walked on stage, dressed immaculately in a custom-fitted, navy blue business suit.

Navy is a power color. Jim knew this. As an introvert, he showed up at this conference overprepared. He doesn't like being on stage, but if you put him there, he'll show up ready to kick some ass.

"Thank you," Jim began, in response to polite applause. He went on to deliver an opening anecdote that reeled in the entire audience. He followed that up by presenting a problem everyone could relate to. Then he offered a creative solution. He wowed everyone with the latest research and technological innovations that backed up everything he said. An hour went by in a blink. Jim walked off the stage amidst thunderous applause.

Boom! Major mic drop.

"What just happened?" Mike gaped. "Are you seeing what I'm seeing?"

"Jim knocked it out of the park," Eddie smiled.

Jim approached his two colleagues, grinning from ear to ear.

"How'd I do?" he asked, feigning ignorance of the accolades around him.

"Jim!" Mike stared at him in disbelief. "You *nailed* it. How the hell did you pull that off? You sit in your cubicle all day. You don't say a freaking word. You don't even come out for lunch. Then *boom!* You turn into Superman. I had *no* idea you had it in you. Great job, man."

"Aw, thanks," Jim replied.

"Not surprised," Eddie grinned. "That's how Jim rolls."

"You knew all along," Mike scratched his head.

"Yeah." Eddie patted Jim on the back. "A guy like Jim, he's not going to look for the spotlight. But if you throw him in it, he'll bring it home."

"Well," Mike chuckled. "This calls for a celebration. I'm heading back to the lounge. Anyone care to join me?"

"I'm in," said Eddie.

"I'm heading back to my room," Jim smiled. "See you tomorrow."

MEETINGS SUCK

Jeremy was a midlevel employee at a well-known department store. Although he's an introvert who wants nothing to do with customers on the sales floor, his supervisor valued him because he brought so many other things to the table, including a unique ability to think outside the box.

During the hiring process for a new general manager, Jeremy's boss put him on the interview committee. There were seven candidates for the job.

It took a while, but the committee narrowed it down to two candidates. And this is where they got stuck. Each of the remaining two candidates had a lot to offer, but in entirely different ways. An extra meeting was scheduled to determine who would get the job for once and for all.

Two hours before the meeting, there was a knock on Jeremy's door.

"Come in," he said.

A young woman walked in. It was Samantha, who worked in a

similar position as Jeremy. Word going around the company was that Samantha was fishing for a promotion. Jeremy was on the interview committee because his supervisor twisted his arm; Samantha willingly volunteered in hopes of showing the organization that she was a good team player.

"Hi Jeremy," said Samantha. "Got a minute?"

"Absolutely," Jeremy replied. "Have a seat."

"Thank you." Samantha cut right to the chase. "It's no secret we're stuck. These applicants are neck and neck. I'm hoping we can wrap this up today. What are your thoughts?"

Jeremy sighed.

"It's not easy," he agreed. "But I think it's going to come down to us deciding whether we want to vote with our hearts or our minds."

"Really?" Samantha shifted in her seat. "How so?"

"Well," Jeremy began. "Tom's the popular choice. He knows this place better than anyone. He could pick up where the previous GM left off and we wouldn't miss a beat."

"But...?"

"I've gone over the files. There's some interesting stuff."

"We've gone over the applicants' files 800 times. Is there something we missed?"

"I'm not talking about the applicants' files. I mean the company files. The analytics."

"Really? How does that affect this?"

"This company hasn't shown any significant growth in four years. Tom worked closely with our old GM. He'll probably give us more of the same. He's the safe choice. But I think we need someone bringing in new ideas."

"And you think Rob is going to do that?"

"I believe he will. I just reviewed his files. He got laid off five years ago."

"That's a plus?"

"He turned it into one."

"You have my undivided attention."

"When he got laid off, he got another job as a temp. They gave him free rein over there. He spearheaded a new marketing campaign and sales went through the roof. I think he can do the same for us."

"That's intriguing," Samantha said. "How come we don't already know that?"

"I'm not sure. I heard someone else took credit for it. But I talked with some people and they confirmed it was all Rob. The whole time they let him do his thing, they did great. Maybe we should give him a similar opportunity."

"Wow. Thank you for your input. Hopefully we'll reach a decision today. See you soon."

Two hours later, Jeremy squirmed in his seat as the interview committee settled down in the conference room. He hated the formality of it all.

"This meeting could have been an email," Jeremy thought to himself. "We could easily do a survey and submit our votes online."

Geoffrey, the interim general manager, called the meeting to order.

"Thank you for your patience," he began.

Jeremy had none.

"Let's try to keep this meeting short and sweet. Would any of you like to share your thoughts before we vote?"

Jeremy's thoughts started percolating. He immediately recalled what he told Samantha about Tom, and his mind simultaneously processed the new information he had dug up on Rob.

Uh-oh. Information overload in progress.

It didn't help that Geoffrey and other VIPs were in attendance, dressed to the nines.

Too many suits. It was visually and mentally overstimulating.

Jeremy took a deep breath and paused, allowing some extra time for his overstimulated mind to unscramble itself. Besides, it was his habit to let one or two other people speak first before he said anything. He needed someone to set the tone, a direction to follow, and then he would be ready to jump in.

Samantha's hand shot up.

"Yes, Samantha?" Geoffrey nodded.

"I'm confident we can keep it short and sweet today," Samantha grinned.

"The floor is yours," Geoffrey replied.

"Thank you. I'll get right to it. We need to make sure we think with our minds, not our hearts. Tom is clearly the sentimental favorite, but Rob brings something we may have overlooked."

Jeremy's eyes shot up.

Hey! She wouldn't!

"If we want to be honest with each other, this company hasn't shown any significant growth in the past four years."

She would!

"I took the liberty of going through Rob's file in more depth," Samantha continued. "It turns out he's had some fascinating marketing ideas that were highly successful when he worked with one of our competitors. So the question is, do we want to play it safe, or do we want to grow? I believe we could use an infusion of new ideas. That's exactly what Rob brings to the table."

Jeremy stared at Samantha in total disbelief. Samantha didn't even look at him. She smiled as the suits nodded their heads in agreement.

How about the irony? Rob was now getting the credit he deserved, thanks to a person who stole credit from Jeremy.

Later that evening, Jeremy tried to make sense out of what happened during dinner with his wife, Marie.

"I don't get it," he said. "Samantha waltzed into my office like she was my BFF. Two hours later, she threw me under the bus."

"Couldn't you call her out?" Marie asked.

"Not in that meeting. Geoffrey's all gung ho about being a team player. If I object to anything, I look like a whiny brat."

"Can you talk to anyone about this?"

"I don't know. Samantha kissed too many asses. I'm too late."

"I wish you spoke up at the beginning."

"Me too. I'm just not comfortable in meetings. I do better one-on-one or through email."

"Then you might want to take advantage of the way you communicate best. Go to your supervisor one-on-one. Tell him you get all these great ideas."

"He knows that. That's why he put me on the committee."

"Great. Now tell him you have trouble expressing those ideas in large groups. Ask him if you can talk privately with him in advance because you have tons of ideas that go unsaid in big meetings. If you share an idea with him alone, will he steal credit from you, too?"

"No, he's not like that. He often tells the big shots that I'm one of his best workers."

"Good. You can share ideas with him. Don't do that with anyone else. At least not alone."

"I still zone out in groups, though. Can't help it."

"That's fine. If you get an idea right before a meeting and your supervisor isn't available, *email* your idea. To everyone. That way no one will steal your stuff at the actual meeting. They'll already know it came from you."

These are great strategies because introverts have the greatest ideas. We just need to make sure we find ways of expressing them from within our comfort zone.

THE BREAKOUT ROOM FROM HELL

It was near the end of a long day at work. Everyone had already mentally checked out. But there was still one meeting left. It was an online workshop on how school staff can do a better job of reaching out to parents.

That's a good topic for an introvert. It's hard for me to reach out to anyone.

The meeting was on Zoom. I clicked on the link, waved a quick hello to everyone, and shut my screen off. I yawned as I watched the presenters.

"A cup of coffee would be really good about right now," I thought to myself. "But hey, they can't see me. Maybe I can catch up on my other work while keeping one eye on the workshop."

So of course, at that moment one of the presenters announced she was sending everyone to a breakout room.

Shit. Now I have to talk to people.

An alert appeared on my screen. It said *Click here to enter Breakout Room Five.* I clicked. There were only four people in the breakout room, including me. I glanced at the screen and smiled. All four of the participants were introverts.

"Well, dang!" I exclaimed. The other participants laughed. No explanation was necessary. We all knew. And because we all knew, we relaxed.

Two of the other participants were support staff for students in my advisory group. The one that just finished 20 minutes earlier.

"Where have you guys been?" I wisecracked.

"I know," said Linda. "It's been so long."

"Well," I sighed. "I'm wiped out. Now I understand how students feel when they're stuck in advisory."

"Actually," said Bill, raising his hand.

Bill rarely talks. This ought to be good.

"Your advisories are great," Bill went on. "Doesn't matter if they're in person or on Zoom. It's awesome. I really enjoy watching you work."

Again, Bill rarely talks. But the fact that he rarely talks made it so much more compelling. He had my undivided attention. This is one of the advantages of being an introvert. When you rarely talk, your words have so much power when you do.

"You teach at the end of the day," Bill continued. "They're *done.* They stare at the screen like zombies."

"Just like we're doing right now," I chuckled.

"Exactly. But you're doing fantastic. You always find a way to make it fun. The kids really appreciate it."

Five minutes ago, I had zero energy. And just now, the quietest person in the whole school lifted my spirits. Bill made my day.

Then we got down to business. We talked about the topic we were assigned to discuss in the breakout room. We had our fair share of quiet pauses, but we also had what was probably the deepest conversation on campus in *years*.

We got interrupted by another Zoom alert. *Breakout session ends in 60 seconds. Click here to return to main group.*

"Time flew," I remarked. The other participants agreed. We bid each other goodbye and returned to the main group.

"Welcome back," said one of the presenters. "Any volunteers willing to share what they discussed?"

A hand shot up. It was one of the more extroverted teachers. She shared what her group had discussed. I watched in awe.

"She's not even looking for words," I marveled. "She just keeps going and going."

This is a common trait of extroverts. They can keep spitting out words without ever running out of stuff to say. This teacher shared an excellent summary of her group's discussion. She might have rambled a bit, but she got the job done.

Oh, and the introverted group? We didn't volunteer any information.

SIDEKICKS FOR INTROVERTS

Prior to a presentation in downtown Philadelphia, I double and triple checked every minor detail. My adrenalin got going as the start time drew near. The auditorium was almost packed and there was a line of people outside still waiting to get in. I quadruple checked my notes.

Why do I always subject myself to this?

I've done this presentation a million times. Each time, it rocks. And I still get the butterflies beforehand. Perhaps more so in front of a hometown crowd.

And then it happened.

Uncle Fred showed up.

Uncle Fred is *that* uncle. The life of the party. The one who knows how to work a room. I had no idea he was going to be at this presentation. In the way that only he can, he got me laughing in no time.

"Hey!" he exclaimed, from his seat in the middle of the auditorium. "I heard this lecture is supposed to be good. What are *you* doing here?"

The tension was broken. Uncle Fred made me laugh, and I fed off his energy. At random parts of the event, we had a little back-and-forth going on. It was one of my best presentations ever.

Now I understand why talk show hosts like having a sidekick.

If you're an introvert who inexplicably winds up on stage, find your anchor. It can be anyone. A dear friend, a colleague, a family member. Look at them, make a connection, and talk directly to them. It'll get you in a relaxed, confident state of mind. The audience becomes a part of this vibe.

The same thing happens at work.

I've been running middle school and high school advisory groups for over 25 years. It's a skill I've developed and refined.

But no matter how good I get at it, one thing remains constant.

I get tired.

I've made it a part of my daily routine to recharge before each advisory. I'll hole up in my office, have a nice cup of coffee, review my notes, and then visualize myself delivering a rock-solid lesson plan. Each time I do this, I turn into *Super Drolz*. At which point I walk into the classroom, raring to go, and have an awesome session.

And then I crash.

At no time during any of this am I being fake with my students. I genuinely enjoy teaching them, and even more, I enjoy learning from them.

At the same time, there's an energy store I have, and its supply is finite. By the end of the day it's completely exhausted. As am I.

My being tired has nothing to do with whether or not it was a good day. After some of my best advisory sessions, you can still find me in a cloud of total brain fog in my office. I'm drained.

As I became more mindful of my introvert tendencies—especially the need to recharge—I noticed something else.

Any time another staff member joins an advisory, my energy doesn't drain as fast as it normally does. There have been times when

I've co-led back-to-back groups with another person and felt great afterward. With a co-leader, my battery remains (almost) fully charged.

That's when I understood what was going on.

I normally work best alone, but in certain extrovert-oriented activities, a sidekick can really help keep me grounded.

Having a sidekick affords you multiple mini-recharging sessions. You collect your thoughts, reassess what you're doing, and adapt if needed. You also get this feeling of having a safety net.

If you brain fart, your sidekick got your back.

Even when you're doing the talking, having a sidekick nearby somehow feeds your energy. More recharging for you.

I have a hybrid car. It goes back and forth between using the gas tank and the battery. The console shows me when the battery is being drained and when it's being recharged. There's a nice balance. That's pretty much me when I have a sidekick.

There are times when my sidekick is "on" and has several spontaneous ideas. Whenever this happens, I tell them to run with it. Carpe diem.

Sometimes my partner is "on" more than I am. Sometimes vice versa. On the best days, we're both "on." Either way, we make the most of it. And no matter who is "on" that day, we find ourselves with a surplus of energy at the end of it. There's no introvert hangover.

There's one thing that needs to be emphasized, though. A sidekick helps me out in situations where my energy is most likely to get drained. During a presentation. At a meeting. In a classroom. On a business trip. When I'm a little bit out of my comfort zone, that sidekick is a godsend. That person will pick me up if I fall by the wayside.

But what about the times when I'm in my element? Like when I'm writing a book or creating a new lesson plan?

See ya!

I close the door and pull down the shade. I work alone. I get in a zone and can't be disturbed. I can work for hours on end when going with my strengths. Any person who wants to help me in that environment may actually throw me off my game.

Another caveat before we wrap up this chapter: don't assume that extroverts have a boundless supply of energy. They're human. Sometimes they need a break, too.

It happened with Sean, one of my most energetic coworkers, during one of those days when nothing went right. It was one thing after the other. A classic Monday with a full moon. It was nearly 4:00pm and Sean was stuck in a meeting.

There were some errands I had to run, and one of them took me past the conference room where Sean was visibly fighting to stay awake. I could see that he was *done*.

I walked in. Everyone glanced at me. I didn't care.

"Sean! Dr. Kelly needs to follow up with you. *Now.*"

Dr. Kelly is our on-call psychiatric consultant. When she calls, it's a big deal.

Sean sighed and got up. He trudged out of the room and barely stifled a yawn.

"Dr. Kelly's on the phone?" he asked.

"No," I replied, breaking into a big grin. "Go home. Have a nice evening."

VISIBLY INTROVERTED

"**P**ete, come here for a second," said Frank. "I got a heads-up for you."

Pete is a tech salesman with more than ten years of experience. He's an introvert, but this doesn't hold him back at all. When he works with customers, he sells tech products to one or two people at a time. It's right in his comfort zone.

Customers aren't an issue. It's the staff meetings that get to him.

"What's up, Frank?"

"You're not going to like this," Frank continued. "You know that supervising intern?"

"Alan, right?"

"Yeah, him. Silver-spooned kid. Becomes our boss the second he gets his diploma."

"He's just an intern," Pete shrugged.

"I know. But he walks around like he's *the shit*. He's making the rounds doing performance reviews."

"He doesn't own this place."

"He acts like he does. Sooner or later he *will*."

"Just keep doing what you do," Pete assured Frank. "Your performance speaks for itself."

"It's not me I'm worried about," Frank said. "I heard you're on Alan's list of people he wants to bark at."

"Excuse me?" Pete stared. "I haven't done anything wrong."

"That's the problem. Alan's intimidated by you because you're *too good*. He wants to show you who's boss."

"Geez," Pete sighed. "Thanks for the heads-up. I'll be ready."

Sure enough, Pete got called into Alan's office. And he definitely wasn't ready. Because no matter how much he thought it over, he couldn't think of any way to defend himself.

It's hard to defend yourself when there's nothing to defend.

Pete's mind spun as he mentally rehearsed every possible nitpicky detail.

"Maybe I didn't put the salt shaker back properly in the break room," he thought to himself. *"Or maybe I accidentally refilled the coffee pot with decaf."*

Pete shifted nervously as he knocked on Alan's door.

"Hi Pete," Alan began, gesturing to a chair across from his desk. "Have a seat."

They shook hands and sat down.

"I'm just doing performance reviews," Alan began.

"I see," Pete replied. "I assume you've seen the reports."

"Oh yeah," Alan acknowledged. "No problem there. You've hit your sales... no, wait. Actually, you've exceeded your sales target the past six months in a row. Pretty impressive."

Pete knew there was a "but" coming in 3... 2... 1...

"But that's not what I wanted to talk about."

"Oh?" Pete raised his eyebrows. "What would you like to discuss?"

"Your attitude."

Pete's heart jumped up into his throat. What was going on? Every single employee and every single customer would vouch that Pete was one of the nicest guys in the store. Where was Alan going with this?

"I'm sorry?" Pete replied. "I'm a little confused here."

"Oh, no, no, no. It's not what you think," said Alan. "I'm not saying you have an attitude problem of any sort. I'm just trying to point out that... how should I say it... I need you to be more of a team player."

Pete could feel his face turning red.

"Damn," he thought. "Frank was right. I'm being put in my place for no reason."

Pete took a deep breath and composed himself.

"How so?" he asked.

"Well," Alan began. "It's essential for company morale that we're all team players."

"I can't say I disagree with that," Pete responded.

"Good. Because I want you to be aware of this. I was watching you last week and there were some issues of concern. Minor issues, I assure you, but I want you to be mindful of it."

"Great," thought Pete. "He's micromanaging. Probably counted how many squares of toilet paper I used during my bathroom break."

"Okay," Pete leaned forward. "I'm all ears."

Something clicked inside Pete. He was going to have an answer for whatever Alan threw at him.

"Thank you," Alan began. "Let's start with that presentation last week. Gary and Steve nailed it. You sat in the back row and walked out the second it was over. In the future, I'd like you to stick around and congratulate those guys. They value your opinion."

"I know they do," Pete replied. "I worked on the presentation with them. I helped them rehearse. During the actual presentation, I left the room knowing my job was done. Just so you know, I'm more of a behind-the-scenes team player. But I assure you, I'm a team player just the same."

"Well, yes," Alan stammered. "But about that behind-the-scenes thing. You keep to yourself a little too much. I've never seen you have lunch with the other associates."

"Ah," Pete shook his head. "I see what you're saying. I do like to eat alone. I'm on the floor all morning and at a certain point, I need some time to recharge. Just 30 minutes of alone time and I'm up and at 'em. In fact, if you check my file again, you'll see that I actually convert more sales in the afternoon. My battery is fully charged at an hour when most people are ready to go home."

"Point taken," Alan said. "But this is about visibility. Visibility leads to better morale."

Alan was visibly grasping at straws. Pete wanted to visibly bang his head on the desk.

"But I am visible," Pete interjected. "If you check my time sheet, you'll see my attendance is perfect. If you check my written reports, you'll see they're immaculate. But I guess I'm more of an introvert. I've never felt the need to be visible for the sake of being visible. I prefer to let my job performance speak for itself, and I believe it does."

Slam dunk! Now it was Alan's face that was turning red.

"That's certainly commendable," Alan acknowledged. Then he grasped for more straws.

"But I don't believe I'm making myself clear. Your work is excellent. It's still the team thing I'm concerned about. For example, at the company-wide meeting, you were seen rolling your eyes."

Holy crap! He IS micromanaging!

"I apologize if that offended anyone," Pete replied. "Guilty as charged. Just so you know, it wasn't the meeting I eye-rolled."

"No?"

"No. It was the icebreaker. I'm sorry, but that was a little out of my comfort zone."

"That might be a problem," Alan smirked, pleased at himself for finally finding a weakness.

"If I may," Pete continued, "I'd like to reframe this. Pardon me if I want to *work*. That's what I'm here for. I want to work, and I want to be the best salesman I can be. I believe my work ethic rubs off on the other employees. This is also a part of my being an introvert. I'm at my best when I'm zeroed in on what I have to do. If we're at a meeting and you're giving me specific strategies that will improve my work, you have my full attention. But if we're walking around the room playing a game where we have to find out who else likes our favorite color, I get overstimulated. It's actually stressful. It may seem like I didn't want to be there, but I just wanted to focus on my work. The icebreaker caught me off guard."

Alan shifted in his seat, seemingly looking for another angle to cherry pick. Pete went on the offensive and cut him off.

"Furthermore, Human Resources is always talking about being mindful of our working environment. It has to be inclusive for everyone, and rightfully so. If we're working hard to create a comfortable working environment, we might want to include introverts. There are a lot of things that make introverts uncomfortable. No offense, but you've been asking me to do some of them. It goes against the grain of who I am."

Boom! Mic drop.

This was one of the most powerful, in-your-face comebacks an employee has ever made to a supervisor.

And it happened.

In Pete's mind.

At two o'clock in the morning, when he woke up and tossed and turned the rest of the night. Because none of the above perfect retorts happened when he needed them the most, 12 hours ago in Alan's office.

A suggestion: make it known from the get-go that you're an introvert. During a job interview, they usually ask you to describe your strengths and weaknesses. You can use "introvert" as a perceived weakness and then easily flip it into a strength. Tell them, "well, I'm an introvert. Some people might look at it in a negative light, but it's actually a strength. You'll find I'm hyper-focused and get things done with immaculate attention to detail."

WHEN PEOPLE DON'T GET IT

I t was the last workshop of the week. Everyone had already mentally gone home. But the presenter, one of the most vibrant people in our field, was known for her over-the-top icebreakers.

Public service announcement: never ask an introvert to participate in an icebreaker.

Knowing full well what was in store, I made my way to the back of the room. Another colleague, Stacy, joined me.

I don't know if Stacy's an introvert, but she shares my disdain for icebreakers.

At the front of the room, conference attendees sat at assigned tables, with five or six people at each one. Stacy and I weren't having any of that. We simply grabbed two chairs and sat in the back, as far away from the action as possible.

Sure enough, the presenter announced there would be an icebreaker. Every person at each table needed to work together and—

Who cares? This didn't apply to Stacy or me. We were way back in the Safe Zone.

"Mark! What are you doing back there?"

Oh, shit.

It was my dear friend, Jack. He's known me for more than 20 years. And he still doesn't fully understand introverts. He turned around and waved at the presenter.

"Chrissy!" he shouted.

Oh, no. He's good friends with the presenter, too.

Chrissy stopped in her tracks and glanced at the back of the room. As did all of the people in attendance. Stacy looked like she wanted to crawl under a rock.

"These two think they can get away with hiding in the back," Jack grinned.

"Oh, no you don't," Chrissy laughed. "You two can join table four."

"Come on," Jack nudged. "Over here."

I discreetly gave Jack my *what are you doing* stare in hopes that he could read my mind. I've told him multiple times that I'm an introvert. Perhaps if I could jog his memory enough, he'd switch gears and cover for me instead of throwing me under the bus.

Didn't work. He was totally oblivious to the death stare I had given him.

"Let's go, you two," Jack beckoned. "Quit slacking and get involved."

Long story short, Stacy and I wound up on stage in front everyone. Our group had chosen us to go up there and summarize what happened in our icebreaker activity.

Of course they did.

After the workshop, Stacy, Jack, and I walked toward the exhibit room.

"Uh, Jack," I said. "For future reference, if you ever see me sitting in the back of the room, I'm *gone*. Done for the day. Elvis has left the building."

"Oh, come on," Jack shrugged. "You *rock*. You always find a way to energize a conference."

"I also need to energize myself," I interjected. "I was trying to recharge. Next thing you know, I'm on stage."

Jack still doesn't get it. Five minutes later, someone at an exhibit booth had to take a bathroom break. Jack promptly volunteered us to cover the booth for 20 minutes.

This kind of thing happens all the time.

Even my own wife forgets.

At a family reunion on a remote campground, we had 80 or 90 people camped out in their RVs. Plenty of good food and drinks to go around, and Melanie's family parties with the best of them. I had fun, but I had to be mindful of my energy level. As one of only three deaf people at this event, I needed an occasional recharge both as a deaf person and as an introvert. I did this by retreating to our RV for a break whenever needed.

Out of nowhere, an unexpected guest showed up. It was a cousin we hadn't seen in a long time. Everyone was thrilled, but she had no place to stay.

"Oh, no worries," Melanie began.

I smiled outwardly. On the inside, I was like Steve Carell in *The Office*:

No! God! No! Please no! No! No! Noooooooooooo!

"You're more than welcome to stay in our RV," Melanie smiled.

I have a lovely, caring, thoughtful wife. Who looked out for a dear relative who is every bit as lovely, caring, and thoughtful as her.

There's no way I can kvetch about this without sounding like a selfish bastard. But the fact remains that my Safe Zone was instantaneously converted into an Awkward Zone.

And this is how introvert problems can spiral into introvert hangovers.

We're very self-conscious. We *know* that we function differently, and that it doesn't make sense to people who aren't introverts.

That's precisely what happened at the aforementioned events. Many of the people who *just don't get it* are friends, relatives, and colleagues. They know *me,* the person with a goofy sense of humor who would give the shirt off his back. They don't know *introverted me,* the person who occasionally needs a break. It's a part of me that's hard for extroverts to comprehend.

What person in his right mind turns down happy hour to take a nap in a stuffy hotel room? This guy.

There's another thing that makes it more complicated. In most awkward scenarios, I suck it up. I don't complain. On rare occasions, such as I did with Jack, I will say something afterward.

We need to speak up sooner and more often.

A few months after the conference fiasco with Jack, a former colleague stopped by to visit us at the office. It was Elena, who had worked in my department for ten years before she retired. The subject of retirement came up and Elena mentioned a former administrator who also happens to be an introvert.

"Kathy's enjoying the introvert life big time," Elena said. "She goes to the beach, walks her dogs, reads a ton of books. I've never seen her so relaxed."

"Wait a minute," I jumped in. "Kathy's an introvert?"

"Of course," Elena confirmed. "When she worked here, she never left her office. Just like you."

"But she talked to people all day long!"

"They all came to her. She didn't go to them."

"That's true," I admitted. "I remember how I used to go to Kathy's office and there were always other people waiting their turn. It's like we had to take a number."

"Well, she's done with that. Now she's a full-time introvert."

"Wow," I marveled. "I should have known. I'm an introvert, too."

Elena laughed. Jack rolled his eyes.

"Oh, come on," Jack insisted. "You're not an introvert. I've seen you in action. You're all over the place."

"And I'm exhausted," I replied. "Have you ever seen me eating lunch with anyone? I shut the office door and pull down the shade."

"Yeah, but..."

Jack still doesn't understand.

"Have you seen me in department meetings? I sit in the back and rarely say anything."

"That's *exactly* what he does," Elena added. "He's always saving his energy. Classic introvert."

Thank you, Elena, for having my back.

"There have been a *lot* of situations where I wasn't comfortable and I just sucked it up," I continued. I mentioned some of them. Elena nodded her head.

"I remember that," Elena laughed. "You looked *mortified.* Your mouth said all the right things but your face said *get me out of here.* I'll never forget that."

"I had no idea," Jack shook his head. "I was right there. Didn't see it at all."

"Elena's right," I confirmed. "I was freaking *dying* there, dude."

It was around this part of the conversation where all of a sudden, I felt so relieved. The mask was off. Jack finally got a glimpse of who I really was.

"I'm curious," Elena jumped in. "All of those situations where you weren't comfortable... why didn't you just say something?"

"I couldn't," I confessed. "I felt guilty."

"I know plenty of staff who spoke up when they didn't like an assigned task and they were excused," Elena reminded me. "They *communicated*. Why not you?"

"Because I'm a softhearted, introverted empath who doesn't have the heart to say no."

Truth.

I have improved since then. I've learned how to say no. It saves so much trouble.

There was something else I learned that day.

If you get in the habit of telling the truth, no matter how uncomfortable it might be, it's a huge step in the right direction.

Here's an interesting exercise: have a trusted friend or colleague ask you several difficult questions back-to-back. Answer *immediately*. Don't think about what would be the most appropriate answer. Don't worry about hurting anyone's feelings. Resist all urge to overthink.

Just blurt the answer out. The truth, the whole truth, the hard truth, the "omigod I can't believe I said that" truth.

It's a fun exercise. It feels so damn good. Because once you get comfortable with it, you soon realize that you have just set yourself free.

AN EXTROVERT'S GUIDE TO INTROVERTS

At a monthly company meeting, a CEO had just finished answering Karen's question. Karen thanked him and sat down.

"Any further questions?" the CEO asked. A hand went up in the back. It was Larry. Larry rarely said anything during the typical workday, let alone at large meetings.

"Yes, Larry?" the CEO motioned for him to stand up.

"I was wondering if there's a way we can..." Larry began.

At that moment, Karen suddenly remembered something she forgot to add when it was her turn. She shot back up from her seat.

"Hey, wait," said Karen. "I remember now. What about—"

"Karen!" Sandra interrupted. "Let Larry finish! He never talks!"

Sandra was right. We get to see Larry say something about as often as we get to see Halley's comet.

"Yes, but this is related to—" Karen protested.

"Sit down!" Sandra glared. "I want to see what Larry says!"

Several fellow employees nodded in agreement. The law of supply and demand was in effect. The supply of Larry's public comments was infinitesimally small. The demand to see what he had to say was off the charts.

Larry didn't care. He had already returned to his seat.

"Larry!" Sandra pleaded. "Get back up there."

Larry shrugged. He reluctantly got back up.

"What I was going to say was..." Larry began. He went on to make a brilliant suggestion that knocked the CEO off his feet.

"That's an *incredible* idea," the CEO remarked. "I'll be sure to bring it up at the next board meeting. Thank you, Larry." The entire room burst into applause. Larry sat down, totally nonplussed.

As Larry settled back into his seat, his good friend Eddie slapped him on the shoulder.

"It's about time you said something intelligent around here," Eddie wisecracked.

"I have one good idea a year," Larry grinned. "And that's my quota right there."

Larry was just being his usual self-deprecating self. The truth is, he gets *plenty* of good ideas. Every day. It's just that no one asks. And he's in no hurry to volunteer any unsolicited feedback. This is something extroverts might want to keep in mind during daily business operations. Here are a few tips:

Do some air traffic control just like Sandra did in the earlier anecdote. Introverts don't have a driving need to be heard. If someone talks over them, they shrug and disappear into the background. You never know what you might have missed. Tell Karen to stick a sock in it and let Larry have his moment. You never know when he'll volunteer again.

Then again, introverts are also known for not having anything to say at the very moment you ask a question. Give them a little head start and send out an agenda for your meeting in advance. If you send out a preliminary agenda that says "we need to come up with creative solutions for trimming our budget next month," the odds of an introvert having a good answer greatly increases.

That meeting that could have been an email? Make it an email. Introverts are more likely to send in a good suggestion when they've had time to think it over, type it down, edit it a few thousand times, and then send it in. Especially from the comfort of their own office.

Although these tips are for the work environment, they apply to social events as well. If you're hosting an event, invite the introverts even if they react like you offered to do a root canal. Then follow up. If the social event has a pre-planned activity—such as a Super Bowl watch party or a cornhole tournament—the introvert guest is more likely to feel comfortable as opposed to when it's a large group randomly gathering.

Make sure your event has ample locations for smaller groups to converge. The kitchen. The TV room. A game room. An outdoor deck. When people are split into smaller groups, the introvert feels less overstimulated and is more likely to participate. An introvert might be uncomfortable in a packed hotel lobby, but still find a comfort zone at the pool or at the bar.

Given the right opportunity in the right environment, introverts have a way of rising to the occasion, just like Larry did at the company meeting. The same thing happens at social events. Introverts can and do wind up being the life of the party. And then *poof*, they're outta there.

PART IV
RELATIONSHIPS

RESTING BITCH FACE

Earlier in this book I mentioned John, who inadvertently gave his good buddy the stink eye when he was in desperate need of a recharge. I also mentioned my wife Melanie, who pointed out that sometimes I give off a vibe that makes me appear unapproachable.

As I compiled stories for this book, there were repeated incidents that made me wonder if there was more to this than I initially thought.

"You did it again," Melanie sighed. "Lacey needs help filling out some forms. She's asking me because *you* look like Hannibal Lecter."

"What did I do?" I protested. "I'm just chilling out."

"You look *mad*."

"But I'm not mad."

"Explain that to the kids, then."

"Okay. I will."

It was time to send out a family text. Yes, text. Sometimes I'm so drained that it feels like a chore to round up my own family.

My kids are all above the age of 17. Getting them to do something together these days is like building a snowman out of dry sand. Texting, on the other hand, gets their immediate attention.

I paused before I texted. I had this gut feeling that somewhere out there, someone else could explain this better than I ever could. I Googled *introvert facial expression.*

I hit the mother lode.

There were a ton of articles. Some of the titles grabbed me and pulled me into my phone. One of them was *I'm an Introvert, and This is Just My Face* by Jenn Granneman. There was also a Reddit post with a headline that said *Tired of comments about my facial expressions.* The guy who posted it was an introvert who lamented about people incessantly asking him *"what's wrong."* And, just like me, he insisted there was nothing wrong.

But the real kicker... the best title of them all...

The Introvert Resting Bitch Face.

I clicked on this article and was *hooked.* It was by Michaela Chung at introvertspring.com. She mentioned scenarios where people ask why you're "so serious" or if you're angry when in fact you were just daydreaming. Chung aptly referred to this unintended look as an introvert's Resting Bitch Face.

Jackpot! It's a great article, and I recommend looking it up.

I copied the link to this article and a few other ones. Before sending them to my family, I texted my own introvert disclaimer:

"Mom has mentioned that sometimes I repel you guys with a facial expression that looks like I'm in a bad mood. I want you to know it's not that at all. There's a term for it. It's called Resting Bitch Face. It's nothing more than recharging after a whole day with people who drain my energy. Darren actually calls this 'spending time in the nothing box.' That's exactly what it is. I'm not 'in a mood.' I'm recharging. I may be quiet, but I'm actually a good communicator. If I AM in a bad mood, I can and will specifically explain why. With remarkable accuracy. So if I'm saying nothing, it's actually nothing.

I'm fine. I don't mean to make anyone uncomfortable and I apologize if I have."

Lacey was the first to respond.

"Actually I think u r just planning murder," she texted.

This was in reference to a hilarious illustration in Chung's article. It showed the facial expression of an introverted woman in three scenarios: daydreaming, cooking, and planning murder. In all three scenarios, the facial expression was exactly the same. The classic Resting Bitch Face.

My daughter is a wiseass.

"No, I already disposed of the body," I texted back.

I have a feeling that whenever the kids need something, they're going to continue to ask Melanie.

NONSOCIAL MEDIA

Social media is a double-edged sword. On the one hand, it offers the ideal social life for an introvert.

You can interact with thousands of friends, family, and even random people without ever leaving the comfort of your own home!

You don't even have to say anything. You can just go in there and *look*. You can give a thumbs up or a goofy emoji if you want to acknowledge someone. You get to see everyone you've ever known your whole life without any awkward small talk. If you want to make a comment, you can. If you don't, then *click*, off to someone else's page you go.

On the other hand, there are plenty of times when the Men at Work song *Who Can It Be Now* goes off in your head.

Who can it be knocking at my door? Go away, don't come 'round here no more...

Seriously. People on social media can get in your head like no other.

Maybe you made what you thought was a harmless comment on someone's wall. All of a sudden, you've set the Internet ablaze. Everyone and their brother wants to make a rebuttal. That's fine, but they do it in a way where you feel you owe a response.

To an extrovert, it's a welcome challenge. To an introvert, it's an unwelcome obligation.

Then there are direct messages. Ninety-nine percent of the time, mine are positive. Usually it's a guy who wants to say "hi, I read your book and loved it" or "I had a great time at your presentation last week." I greatly appreciate those and respond to each one.

But here's the weird thing: introverts are known for having an aversion to the telephone. We love our emails, but when the phone rings it's *Who Can It Be Now* all over again.

Who can it be knocking at my door? Make no sound, tiptoe across the floor...

Direct messages elicit the same response. Especially when they're from someone you don't know. Occasionally, there's a message from some guy who says "I need to talk to you about something you said in your book. You need to revise the part about..."

I'm always open to dialogue and love to learn something new, but I'm not going to rewrite three chapters because of something someone didn't like. That direct message is going to sit in my inbox for an eternity.

Then there are privacy issues that arise in social media, where large numbers of people can peek at your personal life.

In person, introverts greatly prefer interacting with small groups of quality friends rather than attending large gatherings. When I'm having a drink with Neil and Colby, I might tell them about the invasive procedure my doctor did last week. At a huge social event, not so much.

It's the same thing in social media. I might post a video of one of my kids hitting a home run so that my relatives in Canada can catch up. But the really private stuff? Not going to.

There are people online who post pictures of themselves literally being wheeled into surgery. Sometimes, pictures of themselves in actual surgery. I did not need to see that gallbladder, thank you very much.

It makes no sense to an introvert. If we're being wheeled into surgery, our thoughts are entirely focused on the procedure and outcome. At no point do we stop and think, "waitaminute, let me get a picture in case Uncle Joe in Ohio wants to see my enlarged spleen." At. No. Point. Whatsoever.

There are certain things an introvert will and won't post, and I'm no different.

What I do post:

Weddings, anniversaries, graduations, birthday parties, sports events, cute pets, funny videos, the occasional political rant, funny or inspiring memes, thought-provoking topics, and recommendations for small businesses in my neighborhood.

What I don't post:

Funerals, personal drama, work drama, legal drama, up-close commentary about people who tick me off, health issues, private get-togethers, and that invasive medical procedure I told Neil and Colby about.

It's a mixed bag. But still, there's much that introverts can gain from social media. It's a powerful tool. From a socialization perspective, it can help you open up and connect with people in ways you might not have done in person.

I can count on one hand the number of good friends I had in high school. Today, I'm connected with at least 30 former classmates. What hits me is the discovery that they're all really cool people. Back in the days when we actually shared a classroom, I had no idea.

Then there's networking. The mere thought of going to a conference, mingling with a large crowd of people you don't know, and trying to connect with a few of them is an introvert's worst nightmare. We don't want to do it. We'd rather stay in our hotel rooms relaxing in the hot tub, reading a book, or watching a movie.

Have you ever been at a conference where some people seem to be there all day long, while others seemingly disappear and reappear at will?

The Houdinis are the introverts heading back to their rooms to recharge.

Social media allows you to network in such a way that you're always recharging. You post something, and then you're gone. A bunch of people are reading your post while you're at a coffee shop somewhere.

People are catching up with you, and you're not even there! How awesome is that?

Granted, there's still a sense of reluctance that may affect introverts when posting on social media. It might not even be reluctance. It may actually be *disinterest.*

When extroverts post on social media, to the introvert it often looks like they're clamoring for attention. It's hard for us to respond in kind.

Most introverts don't want attention.

But the fact remains that social media is a powerful tool. If you're an introvert in a profession where networking is a must, social media is something you can take advantage of. The ball is in your court. It's much easier than being put on the spot in a live interview or squirming uncomfortably in a crowded convention hall. You have the luxury of thinking, writing, and editing a comment before you post it.

And then *poof,* you're outta there.

THE HIDDEN INTROVERT

Ron and Jennifer married at an early age. Ron's a flaming intro-vert. Nonetheless, he and Jennifer somehow found a healthy balance with their lifestyles.

They used to hang out in nightclubs with their closest friends. Ron was perfectly fine with this as long as it was a small gathering. They usually went out with two or three other couples. On occasion, Ron would go out on his own for guys' night out. Again, it would be a small group of four or five friends.

As they got older, Ron and Jennifer grew tired of the bar scene. House parties became the new norm. Later, these house parties mellowed out into house gatherings. Everyone has a drink or two, but no one gets rip-roaring drunk and parties into the wee hours of the morning.

This is the extent of Ron's social life. As much as possible, he avoids large gatherings. In the past, if there was a huge event he couldn't get out of—such as a wedding or an anniversary gala—Ron sucked it up and went. But he had interesting strategies that helped him get through it.

Long before cell phones became a thing, Ron would drag a clunky old camcorder around and assign himself the role of cameraman. While everyone else socialized, Ron stood off to the side filming everything.

The camcorder was a barrier. It was his way of setting up a wall between himself and people he didn't really want to interact with.

"Sorry, I can't be bothered! I'm filming for the newlyweds!"

People accepted this because Ron was actually skilled with a camera. His videos were top-notch. Everyone looked forward to seeing them. Some of his friends even hired him for milestone family events.

Ron also got into the habit of bringing a pipe with him, at least before smoking was banned in public places.

It was the late, great comedian George Carlin who went on a classic rant about pipes. He said that smoking a pipe was an arrogant way of putting a flaming barrier between yourself and other people.

For Ron, it was a survival skill.

After camcorders went obsolete and pipes were outlawed, Ron's willingness to attend big events took a nosedive. His lifestyle changed. He hardly goes anywhere these days.

He didn't turn into a total recluse. Whenever someone visits, Ron is always a gracious host and an excellent conversationalist. On occasion, he and Jennifer still visit some of their closest friends.

This is just something he does, not something he needs. Big difference.

Ron has no problem going weeks without socializing. He's happy coming home from work, cooking a good meal, watching a favorite TV show, reading a book, and hanging out with his dog. In the summer months, he's more into carpentry and riding his motorcycle.

Like I said, this guy is a flaming introvert. A happy flaming introvert.

Jennifer, on the other hand, is a party animal. She rarely refuses an opportunity to go out. Anytime there's an event that Ron isn't interested in, Jennifer goes by herself or with a close friend.

Jennifer goes to fancy restaurants.

Jennifer goes to weddings and bar mitzvahs.

Jennifer goes to class reunions.

Jennifer attends job-related conferences—even though she's retired.

Jennifer loves huge galas in the fanciest hotel ballrooms.

Jennifer is popular with her friends.

Jennifer is always invited to social events.

Jennifer is asked to serve on boards and committees.

Jennifer is... an introvert.

Surprise!

Ron and Jennifer are both introverts. They love the stay at home stuff. It's just that Jennifer also enjoys being social on a different level than Ron.

Just because Jennifer likes to get out of the house doesn't mean she suddenly morphs into an extrovert. She doesn't. She has her own set of Introvert Survival Skills.

All of those events she loves attending? She has a limit. She stays two or three hours and then she's done. If she rode with a friend and leaving earlier is not an option, she finds ways to take small breaks. She steps outside. She immerses herself in smaller group discussions. She takes bathroom breaks. If she's at a hotel conference, she retreats to her room for some private time. She knows her limits, and she honors them.

No two introverts are exactly alike. We all have our own tolerance levels and comfort zones. And that's the funny thing—there are people who have marveled at how long Ron and Jennifer have been together, because they think Jennifer is an extrovert. They think it's impossible for introverts and extroverts to coexist.

My wife Melanie is an extrovert. We've driven each other up the wall many times. But we also know how to complement each other and we know when to give each other a break.

For Ron and Jennifer, it's not an issue at all. They have a lot more in common than anyone may have realized. They make it work. As can anyone who stays true to themselves.

CAVEMAN CONVERSATION SKILLS

I admit it. There was a one-page website, a sales funnel, or whatever you call it, that was meant to draw me in and get me to spend my hard-earned money.

I fell for it.

It was an ebook on how to talk to women.

The ad was geared for sophomoric, desperate males. Quite frankly, it was a turn-off. It gave the impression that women are easily manipulatable creatures who can be attracted via primitive, caveman-like mating behaviors.

I'm married. I'm not a caveman.

I just want to be able to maintain a conversation with my wife.

I swallowed my dignity and bought the ebook.

Melanie and I have this on/off dynamic. Sometimes we have something to chat about. Sometimes we just sit there in silence, watching TV or reading a book.

I did not know that it's okay—even desirable—for couples to be able to enjoy moments of silence together. For whatever reason, I've always felt I'm supposed to be Drolz the Chatty Entertainer.

When I first met Melanie, we hit it off because we were in a safe environment. We were in a dorm laundry room and in the company of others. It was highly informal and conversation flowed. I said some funny stuff and there were no moments of awkward silence. Since it was a small group conversation, there were other people who brought up topics to discuss.

For me, this was like having a steady stream of social cues—social cues that I could build on. Something that someone else said would spark something in my mind that I could add to the conversation. I could also get away with the inevitable moments where I had nothing to say, because someone else was always talking.

It was like other people took turns being my wingman.

And then Melanie and I went out on a date.

Just her and me. At a Tex-Mex restaurant.

Crickets chirped.

I was not a smooth talker. At all. I thought this was going to be our first and last date.

Thirty years and three kids later, we're still together.

And there I was, purchasing a cringe-worthy ebook because I still want to be able to hold a good conversation with my lifelong companion.

The advertisement for the ebook focused on the steamier stuff. It was written in a way that appealed to a much younger demographic. But at the same time, it also turned out that the ebook was written by someone who actually has an impressive background in neurolinguistics. He uses this background to show how people of all ages can improve their ability to connect with others. He did have some good points, even if I didn't like his initial approach.

Long story short: if you're frustrated with your social life and feel the need to improve it, there's nothing wrong with finding a life coach, a counselor, or even an online course that could teach you something new.

If you choose this path, I would highly recommend Michaela Chung at introvertspring.com. If you're an introvert and there are some relationship issues you want to work on, there's no better resource than another introvert who has it figured out.

But I'll cut to the chase right here. The big secret in that ebook? Confidence. And by confidence, I don't mean you have to strut around in a nightclub, offering to buy people drinks.

Buying drinks as a means of getting to know someone is a no-no, by the way. It implies you're not worthy of anyone's company unless you have to literally bribe them for a moment of their time.

By confidence, I mean accepting who you are. Being comfortable in your own skin. Embracing those moments of silence not as something awkward, but as a pause that allows a deeper connection to develop on its own. A deeper connection that needs no words.

Although introverts by nature prefer quiet moments, some of us tend to go into people-pleasing mode when we're in the company of others. This exhausts us even faster and creates a stronger need to recharge.

Instead of people-pleasing and searching for others' approval, search for yourself. Find *you*. What things do *you* enjoy? Do them.

Conversely, what things do you *not* enjoy? Take a good look in the mirror. How many of the things you did today are things you did because it was what others wanted? Stuff that you didn't actually enjoy, but merely tolerated?

Eliminate the unwanted stuff as much as you possibly can. Replace it with things you actually enjoy doing.

Then, and only then, do you visibly carry a different vibe.

And that, not an ebook for cavemen, is what makes you uniquely appealing to others.

GET YOUR STORY STRAIGHT

had a rare day off. No one else was home so I had the entire house to myself. It was Introvert Nirvana. Which meant one thing:

If I don't do the dishes before Melanie gets home, I'm in trouble.

It's a perfectly reasonable expectation for a busy household like ours. Everyone's always coming and going. There's always some errand that slips through the cracks.

The house was in good shape other than a huge pile of dishes in the sink. I knew what I had to do, and I came up with a *plan.*

As an introvert who gets easily distracted, I had to write my plan down. A to-do list always makes the day run smoother. I followed it the best that I could.

Getting the little things out of the way first helps me gain a sense of momentum. I walked the dog, fixed a minor problem with the bathroom sink, and threw out the trash.

I know. Big deal. But it feels so good to check off the boxes on a to-do list.

Then I stepped up my game. Just before going on some shopping errands, I threw some dirty clothes in the laundry. I calculated that they would be done by the time I got back.

Now I'm multitasking. This is huge. I usually suck at multitasking.

Just as I was almost done at the supermarket, my daughter texted me from work. She forgot to pack her lunch. I grabbed a sandwich from the deli counter and dropped it off on the way home.

Now I'm multitasking on top of multitasking. Am I on a roll, or what?

A bunch of other stuff got done. By noon, there were only two things left on my to-do list: pick up my daughter from work, and wash those dishes.

Melanie gets home at 5:00 so I wanted to work around that. I figured I'd work on my book for two hours, do a little nothing, wash the dishes at 3:00, then pick up my daughter at 4:00.

Everything went according to plan. My favorite part was "do a little nothing."

This is the best. Never deny yourself the opportunity to do nothing. Doing nothing is actually a form of doing something. It's good for you.

There's nothing like lying down on the couch and letting yourself completely disconnect from the world. You don't even have to nap. Just lay back, and... detach.

Ahhhh.

"What are you doing?"

Gah!

It was Melanie. She came home right before 3:00.

"Wha-wha-what?" I stammered. "I thought you were coming home at 5:00."

"Okay," she said, with a look that clearly indicated it was not okay.

"No, really. That's not what I meant. I mean, um, I was, uhhh..."

I could not find the words. They just weren't there.

Melanie sighed. She walked to the kitchen.

"No, no, no... that's on me," I said. "I got this."

She gave me *the look.*

"No, really," I insisted. "I swear I was going to do this soon."

"Yeah, right," she replied. She shrugged and went upstairs for a nap. I did the dishes.

I'm a great husband, and yet I felt like an asshole.

Even after I spiffed up the kitchen, I didn't feel better. Until...

The to-do list! Evidence!

I don't need to provide written reports to my wife. It doesn't work that way. But she was exhausted from a rough day at the office, so I figured it was best to acknowledge that. Seeing the to-do list kick-started the short-term memory that had abandoned me earlier. Finally, I had the words.

"Mel... I got a lot done today. There's a to-do list in the office if you want to inspect my fine work. But the point is, I thought you were going to be home at 5:00. I planned to do the dishes at 3:00. Then you surprised me and I couldn't find the words to save my ass."

This time, I got an eye roll and a smirk. I was back in her good graces.

Nonetheless, something bothered me.

Where did the words go when I really needed them? I had a plan. That plan was written down. I got a lot done. Yet when asked what I was doing, I drew a total blank.

It's moments like this that make me question my own sanity. Sometimes people ask me about stuff I already did (or was going to do), or they ask a question that's in my area of expertise. It's stuff I should be able to answer in my sleep. But if they ask in the spur of the moment, sometimes I just can't find the words. You can see the tumbleweeds rolling around in my mind.

This is why I dread the Q&A session after a presentation. I might look like Albert Einstein for an hour, only to have one little question at the end make me look like Alfred E. Neuman.

To my relief, I've found that this is common for introverts.

We're thoughtful. We're introspective. We dig *deep* into our thoughts.

And when we dig deep, where do we go? Into our long-term memory. Which means one thing: when we need our short-term memory, we trip all over ourselves.

Imagine an Olympic diver who's in contention for a gold medal. He nails the first five dives. For his last dive, he does a cannonball. That's me when someone asks a question.

In *Introvert Advantage* by Dr. Marti Olsen Laney, this phenomenon is addressed at length. Laney explains how introverts tend to draw upon long-term memory more than short-term memory. For extroverts, the opposite is usually true. This is why extroverts often find the right words faster than introverts.

It's reassuring to know this. For a long time, I genuinely thought there was something wrong with me.

When we dig into our long-term memory, some information is easier to recall than others. Sometimes we're able to do this on short notice. Other times, it takes a while to get the information we need. A disturbingly long time.

Don't you hate that frustrating feeling when you're absolutely certain you have an answer, but it's not quite there yet?

Perhaps the best way to deal with this is to be open about it. If you're worried you might look stupid, you're going to make it worse. Your brain is already looking for the information you need. Rushing it doesn't work. Just tell everyone what's happening and allow time for your long-term memory to do its job.

I have a good relationship my colleagues so for a while there, I used some self-deprecating humor.

"Just a moment, guys, I'm having a brain fart. I'll get right back to you."

But it's not a brain fart, nor is it something you should explain in depth or apologize for. Just be up front with it:

"Give me a moment and I'll get back to you on this. This is one of those times when I have to really dig in there."

If your colleagues are as awesome as mine, they'll actually grow accustomed to the way you think. They'll know how to give you cues to help recall the information you need.

For example, here's a common scenario:

"Mark, do you have anything you want to add?"

"Actually, yes. I was thinking about that workshop last month. I think… hmmm. Where was I going with this?"

"That workshop last month. Dr. Stevenson? You said she made a good point about language acquisition."

"Yes! That! Thank you. I've noticed that our students do much better when they have…"

Thanks to the colleague who fed me a couple of cues, I was able to contribute to the discussion in real time. Otherwise, I would have sent everyone a lengthy email long after the meeting had ended.

I don't even have to explain myself anymore. My newest, most favorite response:

"Hold on a moment. I'm downloading."

VACATION WITH AN INTROVERT

*M*y extroverted wife, Melanie, is a godsend when it comes to vacations. That's because she *plans* them. Me? Not so much. I'm happy where I am on the living room couch. *Too* happy. A ballgame and a nice cold drink are all I need.

My kids? They're thinking "we got the most boring dad in the world."

It helps to have an extroverted partner who balances things out. I know our kids appreciate it. I always need help with the extracurriculars.

I tend to keep it simple. I'm fun to hang out with at the beach. I'll play whiffle ball, throw a football around, and go boogie boarding. We'll find a nice seafood restaurant, or I'll throw something on the grill myself. I also love walking on the boardwalk, especially at night. Except when it's too crowded. In which case there's nothing better than a late-night walk on the beach. Barefoot, with the waves gently rolling up on your feet.

Then there's the ultimate nirvana: a beachfront balcony. You can just sit there, with the cool ocean breeze gently caressing your skin, as you pop open a cold one and—

"*Daaaad! This is boring!*"

Mom to the rescue. Melanie is the perfect antidote for the boring dad moments. She schedules this, this, and that. When we went to Disney World, she planned and coordinated multiple activities that the kids loved. I would have just booked a hotel room and hung out at the pool.

But don't be fooled by my self-deprecating humor. There are times when the kids *want* boring dad.

"*Daaaad! Mom's trying to make us do everything in one day. Do we have to see another freaking museum? I just want to go swimming.*"

It all balances out.

Then there are excursions with extended family and friends. This gets interesting because Melanie is from Fort St. John, Canada. Most of her family and childhood friends are still way out west. It's a long trip to Philadelphia. And when they do visit Philadelphia, especially for the first time, they all say the same thing:

"*I want to see New York!*"

I get it. A popular magazine once described Philadelphia as a glorified pit stop between New York City and Washington, D.C. It's been said that Philadelphia sports fans are so rabid because they have an inferiority complex. We're in the shadow of New York's exciting night life and (allegedly) superior sports teams. We simply can't compete with New York.

Fawn over New York all you want. I'll take a good old cheesesteak on South Street anytime, thank you very much. But the fact remains that anytime Melanie's family or friends come over, they want to visit The City That Never Sleeps.

This is an introvert's nightmare. Driving to New York City is next to impossible, so we take the train. That's two sets of crowds we have to fight through, one at Philly's 30th Street Station and another at

New York's Penn Station.

Why did New York name their train station after my home state? They probably have an inferiority complex of their own.

Then we sight-see. I don't like it. I don't want to be stuck in a group following a museum tour guide talking about the mating habits of the wooly mammoth. In fact, I have no patience for anything touristy.

See, here's the thing. Extroverts want to visit another city. An introvert's mind is already on another planet.

The last time we visited New York, we went to the Empire State Building. Where we stood in line for a disturbingly long time. Introverts aren't fond of lines. There are too many people standing too close to each other. It's overstimulating.

Speaking of overstimulating, somewhere inside the Empire State Building there's a Virtual Tour Simulator. It simulates a helicopter tour of New York. You sit on this moving platform in front of an 18-foot high definition screen and strap yourself in. The platform moves, sometimes jerking violently, in sync with the action on the screen. As soon as I got on that thing, a realization hit me.

I have manboobs!

I jiggled like I never jiggled before. But seriously, it was fun. That was the one time a long line was worth it.

Introverts tend to be more aware of personal boundaries. If you're in a long line and you're standing six inches away from someone, you'll be able to tell if the person is an introvert or not. Introverts are more protective of their personal space.

That guy who was breathing down my neck? I whipped out my phone and played Don't Stand So Close to Me. *He got the hint.*

Then we went to the Statue of Liberty. Interesting. The lines still bothered me, but the ferry ride was actually kind of nice. I liked sitting down, feeling the cool breeze as the boat made its way to Liberty Island, and enjoyed the open spaces once we got there. It was like a nice nature walk. Until we got squeezed like sardines inside Lady Liberty.

For a while there, I thought I was done with New York City. And then...

Hey! Central Park!

My overstimulated, run-down battery recharged immediately. The sights, the scent of the fresh green grass (and maybe some other kinds of grass), and plenty of open spaces. It was like a walking meditation.

When you're not stuck in a long line or bound to an itinerary, it unlocks your mind. The veil is lifted. You're able to appreciate your surroundings. Freedom!

The same thing happened when we visited Los Angeles. The airport, the traffic, and some of the sight-seeing locales were exhausting. But Runyon Canyon? I hiked that thing all day. It was awesome. Ditto for Venice Beach.

An introvert doesn't have to stay home while everyone else is out and about. Everyone has a different idea of what constitutes a good time. Just balance it out. It'll work.

ALL RIGHT, ALL RIGHT

In American Sign Language, the sign for "all right" involves running an open hand across an open palm—the top hand is perpendicular to the upward-facing palm and moves up slightly when crossing over it. This motion is usually done twice, in sync with the two words.

"Are you all right?" and "That's all right" is pretty much what this sign means, depending on the context and your facial expression.

My late grandfather, Mike Novak, took this sign and adapted it. Rather than using two hands, he just lifted one open hand and did the repetitive "all right" motion higher in the air, all the while mouthing "all right, all right." Now the context was entirely different:

"It's all good," "You only live once," and "What the hell, why not."

Mike often did his customized version of *all right, all right* whenever close relatives snuck bottles of Crown Royal into the assistive living facility where he lived. There would be an *all right, all right* followed by the clinking of shot glasses and a big swig.

You could make a case that "all right, all right" also means "down the hatch."

This piece of ASL slang became commonplace in my family.

"All right, all right," my dad once said, when he noticed I had a throbbing hangover after my first college party. "You're in college now."

Several decades later, my wife and I put a different spin on *all right, all right.*

All the way through our thirties and forties, we regularly attended deaf events where we could enjoy the company of our lifelong peers.

Melanie is an extrovert and I'm an introvert. It wasn't that noticeable in the beginning. Ironically, I'm way louder than Melanie at parties, and far more likely to make an ass out of myself. But the fact remains: I'm still an introvert. Which means that no matter how loud I can get, it's only a matter of time before my battery runs out.

Melanie, on the other hand, can talk all night. She actually picks up steam when the clock runs past midnight. The socialization energizes her.

I was able to hang in there the best that I could when we were in our thirties. But in our forties? Age caught up to me. It's hard to fake it when you're an old fart.

A pattern developed. We'd both show up at a party around 7:00pm, raring to go. We'd go our own separate ways and catch up with our own separate groups.

We're not that couple that's joined at the hip. We just bump into each other every half hour or so, occasionally participate in the same conversation, and then we go on our own way again.

At 11:00pm, Melanie's smile still lights up the room.

Me? I'm starting to yawn.

At 11:30, I'm actually getting uncomfortable. My conversation has dried up. I got nothing. I'm out of gas. I want my bed.

I find Melanie at the other side of the room. Her eyes are lit. She's enjoying this party as much as she did almost five hours ago.

Me? I'm done.

I try to discreetly inform Melanie that I want to go home, without insulting the host of the party.

"Can we leave soon?" I sign, out of everyone else's line of sight. "I'm ready to go."

"Yeah, soon," Melanie replies, in a way that indicates "soon" could be another hour or two.

Melanie keeps talking. The clock goes past midnight. I make eye contact with her and raise my eyebrows, hoping she can read my mind.

"Mark!" she smiles. "Can you get me another drink?"

Shit.

It's hard for introverts and extroverts to be on the same page. We needed a *plan.*

I hatched a good one right before the next party.

"Okay, here's the deal," I told Melanie. "I'm not extroverted like you. I'm going to run out of gas. We need a signal where I can tell you it's time to get out of there. A secret signal that only we understand, so it doesn't offend anyone."

"And that signal is?" Melanie sighed.

"The signal is *all right, all right.* If I come up to you and sign *all right, all right,* it means I really want to go home. Out of gas. Done. Ready to hit the sack."

"You're getting old."

"Yes, I am," I agreed. "So do we have a plan? All right, all right?"

"All right, all right," Melanie confirmed.

Later that night, we had a great time. Like clockwork, I ran out of gas at the four-hour mark. I wandered up to Melanie, who was smack in the middle of a conversation with five other people.

Time to put the plan in action.

"All right, all right?" I signed to Melanie, as I gave her a quick hug and a romantic peck on the cheek.

To the casual observer, *all right, all right* took on yet another entirely new context. It looked something like *"how's everything?"* or *"can I get you another drink?"*

Melanie picked up the signal. She nodded, gradually backed out of the conversation, and grabbed her jacket. Soon we were on our way home.

It works!

We're in our fifties now. Things are a little bit different. When you get to that age, you lose your ability to care what other people think. I no longer fake it. I have told my friends point blank that I'm an introvert. They know. They get it.

At the most recent party we went to, I walked up to Melanie again right before midnight.

"All right, all right?" I signed. Then I glanced at our dear friends Katie and Joe. "That's our secret code for *let's get the fuck out of here*," I candidly told them. They laughed. Not only did they appreciate the candor, *they* did the *all right, all right* sign when they were ready to leave.

I have great friends. It has reached the point where just about all of us sign *all right, all right* when it's time to go.

And there you have it: if you're struggling at parties, come up with a code word to get out of them. Better yet, be open about who you are and how you roll. Your true friends understand.

THE BIG TEST

At the time I started working on this book, I thought I had more than enough information to work with. But the further I got into it, the more I realized I needed to do more research.

Introverts are so misunderstood, they even misunderstand themselves.

I wound up reading books by other introverts and found myself learning things I never knew before. One such piece of information is the fact that introverts tend to rely on long-term memory when recalling facts or answering questions.

This was a huge confidence boost. Prior to learning about this, I actually thought there was something wrong with me. There have been so many occasions when I couldn't answer a question in real time. I'd make a fool out of myself in meetings and then come up with the perfect response at 4:00am.

I hope this book helps you as much as it has helped me. I've learned so much. A lot of it is summarized in the cheat code at the end of the book.

Most important though... *does this stuff work?*

In terms of self-awareness, the answer is yes. It feels good to know you aren't obligated to act like an extrovert. The moment you let go of trying to be what others think you should be, you've won the ball game.

But what about *out there?* In that cold cruel world out there, the one outside of your comfort zone, where not many people get it?

Right before this book got published, there was an opportunity to find out. My employer hosted a huge gala in a fancy hotel ballroom packed with 500 people.

It was time to walk through the fire.

Disclaimer: never force yourself go to an event if you have no interest in it. There's nothing wrong with saying "no thanks, that's not for me." In my case, I was both eager and anxious. I wanted to be a part of this milestone event, and at the same time I was wary of the uncomfortable extrovert moments. The survival skills applied here are not meant to be a lifestyle. Instead, they're just a means of getting through an evening that has the potential to be a great time or a total train wreck.

Let's see how it went.

The gala started at 5:00. Melanie wanted to leave the house at 4:00. I stalled. Anyone who showed up before 5:00 would have to wait in line in the lobby until the doors opened. That would have been awkward. We left a little later than planned and got there at 5:15. We blended in immediately. There was no awkward standing in line with random people we didn't know.

Crisis averted.

Socializing was not a problem. At this gala, just about everyone there was either connected to my job or worked in a similar field. I knew in advance that there would be no shortage of people I could connect with for some genuine conversation.

So far, so good.

The first part of the evening was in a hotel atrium where cocktails and appetizers were served. It was nice, but It was standing room only. We were stuffed in there like sardines. Not an ideal environment for introverts.

Uh-oh, here we go.

I felt overwhelmed by the sheer busyness of the room. There were hundreds of conversations going on at once. I felt genuine discomfort. Not good.

This is common for introverts. It's not shyness. We are literally overstimulated in large crowds. We get an introvert version of brain freeze.

Melanie and I moved to the side of the room and wound up chatting with a dear friend from out of town. There was so much to catch up on. Which was a good thing, because I was now locked in. The one person doing the talking helped me block out the distraction of the other 498.

Our conversation somehow went in the direction of genealogy. As fate would have it, a distant cousin of mine was right behind me. We pulled her into the conversation and there was no shortage of things to talk about.

At first glance, this room looked like Introvert Hell, but I was having a good time.

Then the interruptions started.

"Drolz! Whassup? How you been?"

My little bubble burst. At least four people interrupted for a hug and a how-ya-doing. All of them were people I genuinely like. But as a hyper-focused introvert with the attention span of a flea, I was once again overstimulated. I had another episode of introvert brain freeze.

Am I being rude by bailing out of this conversation with Lisa to say hello to Michael? Did I appropriately acknowledge Michael before Jerry snuck up and gave me a bear hug? Can I even finish one conversation here? Gaaaaah!

I glanced at Melanie. She was still locked in on the original conversation we got into when we first arrived.

Me? I was like a hot air balloon that was accidentally untethered. I drifted off aimlessly with no idea where I was going.

I needed something to get grounded again.

The bar!

I made a quick retreat and ordered a drink. While I was there, I bumped into a former colleague I hadn't seen in years. I was able to catch up with him and noticed that my positioning made a big difference. The only thing behind my former colleague was the bar. I was able to focus on him without being distracted by the huge crowd behind me.

Soon an announcement went out that the ballroom was open and dinner was about to be served. As the doors opened, everyone filed in. Except for my old buddy and me. It was just us, alone in the atrium. A third person, also a former colleague, happened to see us and joined our conversation.

In this case, three was not a crowd. With all of the other people out of the way, this was actually a nice, relaxing conversation in what was now a wide-open space. I could breathe and was much more relaxed.

Once we were done catching up, we entered the ballroom and sat at our respective tables. I rejoined Melanie and said hello to everyone seated with us. Most of them were people I knew well. This was by design. Most of these people were also introverts. Also by design.

See where this is going?

One of the introverts sitting with us went out of her way to make seating arrangements beforehand. We were the introvert table. Another person with us deliberately chose to sit at our table instead of with her husband, who was seated at a VIP table. She didn't want to schmooze with the big shots. She preferred to stay in her comfort zone. It was our safe space and we had a system. We'd circulate and say hello to as many people as we could, and when our energy ran low we returned to the introvert table.

We didn't need to set any such ground rules in advance. It's just how we roll and it's what we instinctively did. It worked. We had great food, great drinks, great company, and a home base to return to whenever we needed a quick recharge.

But there were still moments when I felt overstimulated.

So many people to talk to! Where to begin? There's Larry. There's Frank. There's Joe. There's Kate. There's Monica. There's Dave. There's 8000 things to talk about. Uh-oh, mental gridlock. I got nothing.

That's when Mother Nature called. I took a bathroom break. Outside of the ballroom, I bumped into two of my closest friends. We were able to have the kind of conversation we would have got in trouble for if it happened in front of a larger group.

There would be more fun moments. My department got together for some pictures. We hammed it up and grabbed some much need-ed out-of-the-office quality time with each other.

Four hours went by pretty fast. But there was still an hour left, and at this point my battery was nearly drained. I sat down at my ta-ble and just took in the sights around me. I enjoyed the conversation going on without necessarily participating in all of it.

At the introvert table, all conversation is voluntary. We understand.

At 10:00pm the event was officially over, but that didn't mean anyone was leaving. Especially Melanie, who was still going strong with a conversation at another table. I walked over and executed our most reliable exit plan.

"All right, all right?"

Melanie nodded and reached for her jacket.

All right!

But this was a huge deaf event. I don't think there's any event tougher to close down than a deaf event. New conversations sponta-neously popped up on our way out the door. We kept bumping into people, and they kept talking.

The infamous Deaf Goodbye takes an eternity.

After the initial *all right, all right* got us out of the ballroom, there were subsequent conversations at the doorway, in the atrium, in front of the elevator, and in the lobby.

At this juncture it was 10:40. That was 40 minutes of *all right, all right.* I needed a new strategy. I was also mindful that the free parking for this event was only good up until 11:00. I had to move fast.

Melanie was still in deep conversation with two other people when I just leaned over and rummaged through her purse. The contents of her purse jingled until I finally pulled out what I was looking for. The car keys. Melanie gave me a weird look.

"I'm not paying for parking," I shrugged.

Everyone checked their watches and realized I had saved them 20 bucks. We were finally out of there. What could have been an uncomfortable evening was actually quite enjoyable. You can find ways to make it work.

All right, all right?

ODD COUPLE

People have questioned whether or not introverts and extroverts can coexist in long-term relationships. Introverts go out of their comfort zone in an extrovert-driven world with extrovert-driven rules and behaviors. We interact with extroverts in school, at the workplace, and at social events.

So how on earth are we supposed to go home and deal with another extrovert when we're in serious need of a recharge? Meanwhile, the extrovert is raring to go out for dinner?

I can see how two extroverts can be lifelong partners. They can go out and paint the town red as much as they want. Likewise, two introverts can be perfectly content to curl up on the couch with a bowl of popcorn and watch a movie on TV.

A lot of people, extroverts included, don't mind that popcorn and movie at all. But eventually, they're going to want to get out of the house. Two introverts, on the other hand, could binge watch all of the Star

Wars, Star Trek, and Marvel movies for weeks on end. I should know. I've done it.

I'm an introvert married to an extrovert. Some people say that's a recipe for disaster.

Nah.

Melanie leaves the toilet seat down. I leave the toilet seat up. So what?

Melanie likes margaritas. I prefer beer. So what?

I say "that's gross" when Melanie watches Grey's Anatomy. *She says the same thing when I watch* Impractical Jokers. *So what?*

See where this is going?

I'm an introvert and she's an extrovert. So what?

There are times when our personal tastes clash. But there are times when *every* couple's tastes clash. That's life. You communicate, you deal with it, you find a happy medium. Balance.

It's not as hard as it sounds. There's this misconception that introverts greatly prefer to stay home and never go anywhere. Let me clear that up right now.

We have the *ability* to never go anywhere. When we were told to stay home during the COVID-19 lockdown, we shrugged and said *"okay, sure."* It was not a problem.

But do we *want* to never go anywhere? Not necessarily. Many of us enjoy going out. It's just that we have a finite amount of energy for that. It happens to be less energy than an extrovert has. Due to our different responses to dopamine, an introvert's energy may decrease faster while an extrovert's may actually increase. Either way, once that energy is used up, it's time to go home.

When Melanie and I go to social events, my window for having a good time is usually two to four hours. At which point I start signaling her with our trademark *all right, all right* escape code. Then we either leave, or I sneak out on my own and Melanie stays longer.

So what? If Melanie stays eight hours and I stay for four, that's four hours of a good time we had together. If she wants more, that's her pre-

rogative. I'm hauling my ass to bed. It's all good.

Furthermore, even though there are inevitably moments of conflict, I still think there's a yin-yang dynamic that makes the introvert-extrovert pairing work.

Sometimes, an introvert can protect an extrovert from themselves. Extroverts thrive on dopamine. They can overwork themselves to a point of exhaustion and not even know it—at which point an introvert can intervene and show the extrovert how to recover from overwork (or overpartying).

Conversely, sometimes introverts need to be drawn out of their comfort zones. Earlier in this book I mentioned Linda Baine, a kind soul who went out of her way to recruit me for a job at the Pennsylvania School for the Deaf. At the time, I was a supermarket clerk who was *too satisfied* with his safe space in the toothpaste aisle.

Linda had to visit the store multiple times to get me to agree to a job interview at PSD. She told me, over and over, that a new life was out there for me. She was right, and yet I was resistant. As an introvert I had no desire for any thrill seeking of any kind. It didn't matter if it was a new job or skydiving. I had no inner desire for any dopamine-inducing activity.

My life was nice, safe, and *boring.* The boring part never bothered me. I never woke up one morning and spontaneously said, *"hey, maybe I'll go skiing today."*

But I did have a good buddy in high school who said, *"hey, Mark, have you ever gone skiing? No? Are you serious? Damn. Come with me next Saturday. You'll have a great time."*

I went with him the following Saturday, and I had a great time. A great time I never would have sought out on my own. Sometimes we need that extroverted person to show us there's more out there than we realized.

Which is precisely what Linda did when she pulled me to PSD, a move that totally changed my life for the better. It's also what Melanie did for me (and our whole family) when she coordinated vacation excursions to Montreal, Toronto, Los Angeles, San Diego, Orlando, and many more.

It rubs off on the introvert. I've since planned and gone on trips to Utah, Colorado, Ontario, and others. I've learned how to search for exciting things that don't conflict with my introverted nature. I can travel to a beautiful locale. Just don't ask me to visit a crowded touristy spot where you have to wait 30 minutes for a cup of coffee.

So yes, an introvert and an extrovert can make it work. We always find that balance.

During a trip to Washington, D.C., Melanie and I had a busy (and for me, exhausting) day seeing all of the sights and attending a work-related conference. As we settled into our hotel room, I was ready to kick off my shoes and chill out in front of the TV. I also sensed that Melanie might be hungry.

"Would you be interested in dinner?" I asked. Her eyes lit up.

"Yes, I'd love a good dinner."

"No problem," I smiled. "I got this."

I picked up the phone.

"Hello, room service?"

THE HANGOVER FROM HELL

Class reunions are complicated. Even extroverts balk at them. But for the introvert, deciding whether or not to attend a class reunion is like driving with one foot on the gas and the other on the brake.

There's an old friend or two that you haven't seen in decades. You're excited to see them again. *But wait! There are going to be a lot of other people, too. Crowds suck.*

You'll enjoy a nice, nostalgic walk through the halls where you got your education. *But wait! A lot of other people are going on that walk, too. You'll find yourself making awkward small talk with someone whose name you can't remember.*

There's a huge dinner event celebrating your class. Awesome food and drinks. *But wait! That dinner event is six hours long. It's one of several events planned back-to-back with hardly any breaks. There's not much opportunity to recharge.*

Melanie and I went to a recent class reunion. There was no doubt that she and I, in our own introverted and extroverted ways, were going to enjoy ourselves. But I needed a *plan* to get through it.

One way you can get through a long day is to compartmentalize it. When you get through each part, you feel a sense of progression. You can see the light at the end of the tunnel. It prevents you from feeling too overwhelmed.

I can't emphasize enough that I can and do enjoy these events. It's not like Melanie drags me kicking and screaming to them. It's just that as an introvert, there are going to be moments when I run out of gas. All I need is the occasional chance to retreat and recharge. Then I'm back out there being my mischievous self.

We arrived at our class reunion on a Friday afternoon. There was a huge luncheon in the cafeteria. Not a problem. Why? Because it was a lunch featuring several guest speakers and performances. I let myself off the hook by telling myself that at this particular time, I was nothing more than a spectator. No need to put on an extrovert mask or anything of the sort.

That's right. Just sit back and enjoy the show.

The show went on a bit longer than expected. Again, no problem. I sneaked out. My son, Darren, attends my alma mater. He's on the baseball team. I went over to the field and surprised him at practice. Hung out with his team for a while and talked baseball.

Doesn't matter that I'm an introvert. I can talk baseball for an eternity.

Feeling refreshed, I went back to the cafeteria and rejoined Melanie at our table.

"Where'd you disappear to?" asked one of the other guests.

"Cafeteria food hasn't changed," I replied. "It still sends me running to the bathroom." After some scatological humor, we redirected our attention back to the festivities.

So far, so good.

Next was the campus tour. We got to visit all of our old haunts, and that wound up being a lot of fun. When you're walking around outdoors, it's like a relaxing walk in the park. You're not stuck in one place.

We had dinner on our own with a small group of friends. Quality friends. The people we hadn't seen in decades and were excited to see again.

This was turning out to be a great weekend, after all.

After dinner, Melanie and I retreated to our hotel room. I took a nap.

Recharge! Battery back at full strength.

Next was an evening out at a local nightclub. We had a great time. By midnight, my energy started running low. No worries. We went back to our hotel.

Once again, full recharge.

Saturday was more of a challenge. There was a parade, a football game, a barbeque, and a ton of people. There were a lot of conversations. I began having trouble focusing because every time I got into a conversation with an old classmate, another one would tap me on the shoulder and interrupt. I often lost track of what I was saying.

Uh-oh, introvert meltdown forthcoming.

I retreated to the snack bar and inhaled a bratwurst.

Regroup, Drolz!

Somehow, I made it through the day. I can't even remember everything we did. All I know is it was a mix of fun, busy, exciting, and exhausting. There was not much opportunity to recharge. Melanie and I made a quick retreat to our hotel room to change into formal attire for the evening gala.

I went into the gala knowing that my energy was once again running low. No problem.

Off to the bar!

I'm not recommending alcohol as a solution to anyone's problems. But if you do enjoy a drink every now and then, it does make for a nice social lubricant. I relaxed.

The gala ran for several hours, but I was okay. Again, I compartmentalized.

Drinks. Appetizers. Main course. Presentation. Entertainment. More drinks. Quality time with old friends. All good.

The best part? The gala was in the same hotel where Melanie and I stayed. Our room was just an elevator ride away. Next thing you know, I kicked off my shoes and plopped down on the bed.

Ahhhhh. Made it. I was out like a light. I slept better than I had in a long time.

"Drolz! Wake up!"

"Wuh-wuh-wuh-wut?" I stammered.

It was 7:00am.

"We have breakfast," Melanie replied.

"With who? For what?"

"Ronnie and Laura. They're driving back to Michigan. Let's grab breakfast with them before they leave."

"Wuh-wuh-waitaminute." My body was awake, but my mind had yet to follow. "I didn't know there was an early breakfast."

"It was last minute," Melanie explained. "Steve and Lisa are joining us, too. We don't know when we'll get to see Ronnie and Laura again. Might as well grab some time with them before they leave."

"Yeah, but..." I rubbed my eyes, trying my best to shake off some lingering brain fog. "This caught me off guard."

"Drolz, let's go," Melanie nudged. "Ronnie and Laura want to be on the road by 9:00. We need to leave now."

Normally, this breakfast would have been fine. But the class reunion festivities had gone on for two entire days. I was wiped out. Once the gala was over, my nice, fluffy hotel bed was waiting for me. I let go and fell into a deep, refreshing sleep. When Melanie woke me up, it was like Bam Margera in Jackass. *He woke his parents up in the wee hours of the morning with fireworks in a trash can. Melanie might as well may have done the same thing.*

This was one of those times when my introvert brain and Melanie's extrovert brain were not on the same page. Not just mentally, but literally *biologically.* Introverts are sensitive to dopamine. Extroverts thrive on it. Melanie was in a place where the thrill of another get-together stimulated her mind. She was thinking *let's go! More fun!*

My mind was in a different place. I was thinking *oh my god. I got nothing left.*

Of course, I enjoyed breakfast with my friends. I love them. At the same time, I needed two cups of coffee just to become coherent again. I figured a jolt of caffeine would have me back up and at 'em.

It did, but it was short-lived. Something happened on the ride home. I turned into something I'd never been before.

A diva. A steaming hot mess of a diva.

I complained about the guy in front of me driving too slow. The guy behind me driving too fast. I was hungry. The food we picked up at a convenience store tasted like cardboard. The Baltimore-Washington Parkway has been under construction since 1947. I was tired. We could have checked out of the hotel at 11:00am. Who in their right mind checks out three hours early when we could've easily had a few more hours of sleep on that nice, fluffy, bed? Our mattress at home feels like it's stuffed with bowling balls.

I was spiraling. That Resting Bitch Face that introverts are known for? Mine had upgraded to Active Bitch Mouth. I could not shut up.

I was entering that dangerous territory where my marriage could be in trouble.

I stopped complaining about everything under the sun, but we weren't out of this yet. My behavior veered off in an entirely new direction, one that was still off the rails.

I began to question what I'd done with my life.

It's normal to meet people at class reunions who have accomplished more than you have. The ones who are humble are inspiring, and the ones who brag are annoying. Either way, sometimes you wind up questioning if you could have accomplished more, too. The woulda, coulda, shoulda starts picking at your brain. In this instance, it was like getting smacked in the face with a two-by-four.

"What's wrong with me?" I asked Melanie.

She could have easily taken a few hours to answer that, but she took the high road. She just shrugged and let me go on with my rant.

"My fourth-grade teacher said I could be a writer," I continued. "Mrs. Paul had me figured out long before I had me figured out. I should have listened to her. Why didn't I do anything?"

"You know what?" Melanie responded. "Maybe next time, I'll go alone. You can stay home and write. Knock yourself out."

"No, that's not it," I insisted. "I really did have a good time. It's just that I need *balance*. More breaks in between activities."

"Sure," Melanie shrugged. "But you really went off the deep end this time."

"I know," I admitted. "I'm sorry. This was bad even for me. It's just that my battery got so drained on Saturday, I had nothing left for Sunday. Hey, waitaminute!"

I made a mental note to look for an article when we got home. I needed Melanie to know that I hadn't lost my mind.

I found it. It was an article by Jenn Granneman. *12 Signs You Have an 'Introvert Hangover' (Yes, It's Real).* In this highly validating article, Granneman cautions that "it's not that you don't love your family. Some parts of the day were actually fun. But after so much socializing, you feel like you've run a marathon."

Preach, Jenn!

Granneman goes on to explain that if you experience this, there's nothing wrong with you. You simply have an introvert hangover.

Of the 12 signs she describes in the article, the first one perfectly explained my meltdown in the car: *Every little thing is getting on your nerves.* "It's not unusual for even very loving couples or friends to get into vicious fights when one of them is socially exhausted," Granneman remarks.

I'm off the hook. I think.

The ninth sign in Granneman's article also hit home: *You feel depressed.* People with introvert hangovers can "find themselves being overly pessimistic and cynical, and they question decisions they've made in their life."

Now we know why I asked myself how come I didn't listen to my fourth-grade teacher.

It's a great article. Look it up. I have two takeaways from that literary classic.

One: Introverts, if you've burned out, you don't have to apologize for it. Your feelings are real. Right or wrong doesn't matter. They're *your* feelings, and there's good reason you have them. Be true to yourself. If you enjoy these events, go to them. If you don't, then don't go. If you enjoy them but flame out like I did, communicate with your partner. Find that balance.

Two: *Jenn, if you're reading this, thank you for saving my marriage.*

PART V
SELF-AWARENESS

SELF-CARE: ARE YOU KIDDING ME?

There's a cheat code at the end of this book. Most of the tips and strategies were already in mind before I started writing. Some of them popped up at the last minute. Even though I'm an introvert myself, there were some new things I discovered on this journey.

For example, I was thrilled to learn that my tendency to draw a blank in department meetings has nothing to do with brain fog. Instead, it's based on the scientifically-proven fact that introverts depend on long-term memory to process their thoughts.

We're not slow. We're deep.

Being aware of this helps us come up with solutions. Now we know it's a good idea to prepare in advance for department meetings. As for the inevitable moments when something catches us off guard, we can still have a ready-made response. We can just come out with it and tell our colleagues we need a little more time to process our thoughts. It's all good.

The science and the psychology are fascinating. I enjoy researching both.

Then I looked up some articles on self-care.

Are you kidding me?

Self-care is a big thing these days. A lot of people recommend it. I get it. It's just that a lot of the suggestions garner an eye roll. Here are some of them from an online article:

Take a bath. Go outside. Read. Take a nap. Get a massage. Listen to music. Write poetry. Read poetry. Find quiet time. Draw or paint. Talk to a friend. Do crossword puzzles.

The first thought that crossed my mind when I read that article was *this must have been written by Captain Obvious.*

Workshops on self-care are more of the same.

Let's get real: I would rather take care of myself than spend three hours listening to someone tell me how to take care of myself.

But you know what? Once you get past the initial eye roll, you'll see that most of the seemingly inane suggestions aren't wrong. They might sound silly, but they absolutely work. Even if you feel like saying *well, duh.*

We have to be told the *well, duh* stuff because for whatever reason, it's as if we need *permission* to do them. We live in an extrovert-biased world. Sometimes we have to put on an extrovert mask when we're out and about. We feel pressure to conform.

You'll find some well, duh *in the cheat code at the end of this book, too. You're welcome.*

So yes, *duh,* of course a nice bath sounds great.

The hard part is knowing it's okay to turn down a night at the club for a night in the tub. All of the Captain Obvious self-care tips are nothing more than a band-aid if you aren't genuinely in tune with who you are.

Stay home if you want. It's fine.

SAYING No

One of the most important skills an introvert can have is the ability to say *no*. It's our lifeline. While we can and do enjoy participating in extrovert-oriented events and activities, we all have our limits.

Some introverts need to make more of an adjustment than others. We can learn how to make small talk or redirect it into something more appealing. We can go out for a night on the town, but with an escape plan ready if we need it. We have strategies than can help us get through any social situation, large or small.

Some introverts have no issues whatsoever in the extrovert world. There are teachers, coaches, athletes, business executives, and entertainers who thrive on getting out there and doing their thing. You'd never know they're introverts if they didn't tell you. But there's one thing they share with introverts who lead a quieter lifestyle.

We. All. Need. To. Recharge.

To recharge, we need time alone. To have time alone, we need to keep parts of our schedules to ourselves. To keep parts of our schedules to ourselves, we need to say no.

Not all of us are good at saying no.

The first step in learning how to say no is to value yourself. Valuing yourself is the key to your well-being. You *need* that recharge time. If you don't have it, you'll wind up with an introvert hangover.

There's a whole chapter dedicated to introvert hangovers in *The Secret Lives of Introverts* by Jenn Granneman. She has also written about it in articles on her website, and for good reason: if you don't pace yourself and allow some breathing room, this is something that will hit like a ton of bricks.

I've had introvert hangovers at work and at home. I've been discombobulated to the point where I couldn't complete the simplest of tasks. And it hits physically, too. I'm generally exhausted for a day or two after this happens. The only cure is to retreat and recharge.

So again: if you want to avoid the dreaded introvert hangover, value yourself. And how do you do that? Here's a math exercise that may help.

Take note of what time you get up in the morning and what time you go to bed. How many waking hours is that? Okay. Now how many of those hours were spent doing something you really wanted to do?

The formula is simple: hours of stuff you really wanted to do divided by hours awake times 100 equals the percentage of time spent doing what's important to you.

If you're below 50 percent, you might be headed toward an introvert hangover. As an admitted people-pleasing introvert, my *stuff I really wanted to do* level has often been at ten percent or less. Some days, zero. That didn't improve until I learned how to consistently say no.

You deserve to enjoy life the way you want. Extroverts do it all the time.

Why not you?

Of course, extroverts have an advantage. Their brains are literally wired in such a way that they thrive on being social. This may seem unfair to an introvert, because an extrovert's idea of a good time is viewed as socially acceptable whereas an introvert's need for quiet time may be viewed as antisocial.

It's not antisocial. It's called self-care. An introvert's brain inevitably gets overstimulated in social situations and needs to recharge in solitude.

Have you ever seen that old Ultraman series where Ultraman can only do battle on Earth for a limited amount of time before his red warning blinker goes off? Introverts are the same way. Staying home and watching a good movie is just as good as having drinks at the bar with your friends.

Say no.

Enjoy your night in.

RE(HARGING

Recharging is in vogue these days. Everyone's doing it.
With their cell phones.

If anyone gives you a hard time when you opt out of a night on the town, tell them you're just like their phone. What would happen if they never recharged it?

If only people valued recharging themselves as much as their phones.

When I was in school, we actually had a recharge time built into our schedule.

No, I'm not talking about nap time. Although I would absolutely support that.

I went to a Quaker school. I'm talking about weekly meeting for worship.

Once a week, the whole school would convene for an hour in a meetinghouse across the parking lot from the main building. While this was technically called meeting for worship, there wasn't a sermon or anything.

We sat in silence.

If any of us spontaneously felt moved to say something, we did. It was believed that this was an inspiration from the light within.

It didn't matter if ten people got up and said something, or if no one said anything at all.

The silence itself was golden.

During my earlier days as a student, this initially seemed boring. Ridiculously boring. A bunch of people sitting around saying nothing. Unless somebody felt compelled to say something. Then it was back to a bunch of people saying nothing.

Yawn.

But something changed. It grew on me.

The older I got, the more I felt the pressure of daily life. Especially in high school. Homework assignments, term papers, tests, midterms, finals, projects, placement tests, and more. I was in over my head. My mind spun every which way.

But we always had meeting for worship. Eventually the realization hit me:

Our minds are like a snow globe.

Sitting in silence allows the snow to settle. The globe becomes crystal clear. And that's when *it* would happen.

Hey! Mind candy!

First, my mind would calm down. Then *I* would calm down.

If this isn't proof of the mind-body connection, I don't know what is.

During this quiet calm, there would be complete, relaxing silence. And then, out of nowhere, ideas would pop up.

That term paper I had no idea what to do with? All of a sudden, I had a brilliant strategy on how to wrap it up. That history lecture that made no sense the other day? All of a sudden, it came together and I'd ace an upcoming test.

The ideas and inspiration that popped up in my mind didn't always have something to do with school. Sometimes they helped me solve an unrelated problem. Or maybe there would be a deep thought about human nature in general. Mind-blowing stuff.

It's no coincidence that my school's motto was "Behold, I have set before thee an open door." Sitting in silence opened up some doors in our minds.

As someone who has enjoyed the health benefits of intermittent fasting, I'm aware that fasting detoxifies the digestive system. Meeting for worship, or any other form of silent meditation, detoxifies the mind.

When you recharge in silence, the overwhelm from crowded places and overstimulation go away. It's replaced first by a refreshing silence, and then by the emergence of our own thoughts. We are reunited with our ideas, our dreams, our fantasies.

Silence allows us to get back in touch with our authentic selves. We can connect with deeper, universal truths. We can discern our thoughts and feelings from those of another person or society as a whole. This effectively recharges us and allows us to reconnect with the world on our own terms.

That Quaker school I went to? I graduated a long time ago. But I still have my quiet time. So do you. It comes in many forms. It could be sitting on the couch in solitude. It could be driving to work, walking the dog, doing the dishes, and so on.

It's important that you allow time in your schedule for this. In *Quiet* by Susan Cain, there's an anecdote about a renowned lecturer who became physically ill when people made excessive demands on his time. Without any recharge time, he crashed and burned.

Savor your recharge time.

Enjoy being able to hear yourself think.

Watch the snow settle.

PURPLE BRAIN

The first time I ever saw Prince, the multitalented musician best-known for his chart-topping album *Purple Rain*, was on MTV back in the early 1980s. MTV had Prince's *1999* video on heavy rotation.

My reaction? "Whoa, cool. This dude's a badass."

My curiosity was piqued. I had to find out who this guy was. I looked up his previous albums and discovered *Controversy* and *Dirty Mind*.

Whoa, cool. This dude's a RAUNCHY badass.

Prince's next album, the aforementioned *Purple Rain*, turned him into a bona fide superstar.

I've never met Prince so I'm only assuming here, but I think it's safe to say he was an introvert. Getting him to consent to an interview back in the day was next to impossible. He did not seem comfortable at awards shows, except when he was on stage performing at one. He thrived in the limelight and disappeared out of it.

Most likely to recharge.

Fast-forward to today and although Prince is no longer with us, having tragically passed away at age 57, his impact remains as strong as it was that first time I saw him on MTV. I actually try to emulate him as much as possible in my professional career.

No, I do not show up at work in high heels and a trench coat. I'm talking about his work ethic.

I was already a fan before *Purple Rain*. But when Prince released that album, I was awestruck on an entirely new level. He had hit the mother lode. His music, his look, his persona... it was going to dominate for *decades.*

He reacted to that in a way that surprised me. He promptly *changed* his music, his look, and his persona. His next album, *Around the World in a Day*, was nothing like anything he had released in the past. It was an abrupt departure from it.

What the hell?

If Prince had retained the same look and the same sound from the *Dirty Mind–Purple Rain* era, he would have cemented himself, much earlier, as an icon. Perhaps the number one commercial rock star of all time.

He wasn't having any of that.

At the time, being too young to understand his motivation, my reaction to his ever-evolving music was *dude, what are you doing?*

I'll tell you what he was doing. He was marching to the beat of his own drum. He liked to challenge himself with an introspective *"what if I did this differently?"* and he pushed those limits accordingly. To an introvert, taking the road less traveled is mentally stimulating. It's like an antidote for small talk.

Recharging doesn't necessarily mean sitting at home doing nothing. It can also mean working intently, in solitude, at whatever it is that you do best. And challenging yourself to do even better.

Prince wound up releasing 39 albums in his career. It's been said there are at least 50 more unreleased albums in his vault.

I'm not planning to write 39 books. But there are some things

Prince did that I keep in mind when I'm working. It wouldn't surprise me if other introverts are doing the same. Here are some suggestions based on the actions of His Royal Badness:

Always make time for yourself. Early in his career, when Prince and his band were in Orlando during a tour with Rick James, Prince declined an invite from his bandmates to join them on a trip to Disney World. He stayed behind at the hotel, playing his guitar on the balcony. When the band returned, Prince had wrapped up *When You Were Mine*, one of his most critically acclaimed songs.

Strive for originality. Prince was forever changing up his setlist and his songs. His songs kept evolving as he went along. It's as if he never played the same song twice. If he played *Controversy* in New York one week, you can be sure he played a different rendition the following week in Los Angeles.

I have the same mindset. At every single presentation I've ever done, I've added something new that I hadn't done at the one before. The mere thought that one person at any of my talks might have seen me before makes me want to make sure it's still entertaining for that one person.

Incidentally, NBA hall of famer and noted introvert Michael Jordan had a similar mentality during his storied career. He once mentioned how he was mindful that at any given game, there might be a kid there watching him for the first time. That kid deserves the best.

Reinvent yourself. It adds an aura of intrigue and excitement. For a goof, I once did an entire presentation where I channeled my inner George Carlin. Instead of lecturing, I went on a comedic rant. The audience was blown away. It was one of those rare times when I thoroughly loved being on stage. Then I went home.

Speaking of reinventing yourself, there's actually a book titled *Reinvent Yourself* by James Altucher. Check it out and dare to be different. If there's anything introverts thrive on, it's thumbing our noses at conformity.

I'm a high school guidance counselor writing a book titled People

Suck. *Need I say more?*

Dare to do things differently. Dare 2 be U.

EXERCISE: INSTANT RECHARGE

I'm a huge martial arts fan. I have a black belt in Tae Kwon Do. It's something I challenged myself to do when I was 19 years old.

Some people may argue that Tae Kwon Do is not the most practical of martial arts. It includes jumping and spinning kicks that you wouldn't want to use in an actual self-defense situation. I get that. A jumping spinning back hook kick is not a good choice in a bar fight.

There are some Tae Kwon Do masters who will disagree with me. They're elite athletes and I'm not going to mess with them. Either way, my Tae Kwon Do class was not all about sexy-looking kicks. Our classes included basic punching and kicking, advanced kicking techniques, self-defense, weapons, forms, and sparring. When we worked on self-defense, we kept it realistic.

My favorite technique? That sexy jumping spinning back hook kick.

It wasn't about self-defense. The only place that kick worked for me was in tournaments, with plenty of space and a referee calling for time whenever someone scored a point.

So why did I fall in love with a kick that had just about zero practical application?

Because it forced me to face my biggest opponent: myself.

Just because introverts like to keep to themselves doesn't mean they don't like to challenge themselves. When we're lost in our thoughts, our thoughts often challenge us. It's stimulating. We like to come up with new ideas. We like to ask ourselves "what if" and "why not." Then we push ourselves in our own little world.

I signed up for Tae Kwon Do because I wanted to turn my life around. I was in a bad place physically and mentally. Instinctively, I knew that the martial arts would get me back on track. And it did.

During my first week of class, I was in awe of the advanced students. I was just a white belt who could barely do a front snap kick. When I glanced at the advanced students, they were doing all these gyrations in the air, defying the laws of physics with their hang time, and nailing their jumping spinning kicks with remarkable accuracy.

"I want to do that!" I said to myself.

It took a few years to master the basics. It required physical conditioning and mental discipline.

I got there.

Next thing you know, I was airborne. Jumping up, getting some good vertical, spinning in mid-air, and then—*whap!*—striking a handheld target pad with the back of my foot. With the same remarkable accuracy as those advanced students I looked up to.

When you set a goal and accomplish it, you condition yourself to believe. You'll set more goals, and you'll get there.

Tae Kwon Do was not the only thing I challenged myself with. A few years after my training began, I accepted a job as a Resident Advisor at the Pennsylvania School for the Deaf. As mentioned in a previous chapter, this was the first job I ever had that required consistent interaction with other people. You'd think it was inevitable that sooner or later, it would have burned me out. Somehow it didn't. I don't remember ever thinking *I need to recharge* during my first year in that role.

Until...

A freak surfing accident threw out my back. I couldn't do a simple front snap kick, let alone one that required jumping and spinning in mid-air. I had to take a lengthy break from Tae Kwon Do to allow my back to heal.

The difference was instantly noticeable.

"You look off," my supervisor said, with the blunt honesty she was known for. "When you stop doing karate, your affect is different. It's like night and day."

She was right. Without Tae Kwon Do, there was no equilibrium. I didn't know it at the time, but I had an introvert hangover.

And, also without knowing it, I had put on the first public display of my infamous Resting Bitch Face.

It makes sense. First, Tae Kwon Do is cathartic. It gets all of your nervous energy out. You could say the same about lifting weights, running, or any other form of exercise. It's a release.

Second, Tae Kwon Do requires focus. A lot of times, introverts can feel overstimulated by their environment, especially in crowded places. But if you're doing something that requires focus, or a consistent routine, that sense of overwhelm dissipates.

Third, there's a spiritual aspect that often gets overlooked. There's a daily meditation at the beginning and end of class. Then there's the state of *mushin*, also known as *no mind*, that is common in the martial arts and meditation.

I can't even explain what mushin is. But when you experience it, you'll know.

In retrospect, I've been an introvert my whole life and somehow didn't know. My martial arts experience may have masked it.

The whole time I was working out, I was recharging. It kept my energy at a level I never would have been able to maintain on my own.

When you plug in an electric car overnight, it'll go a long way with no problem. When you go to a martial arts class three or four times a week, you'll go a long way with no problem.

In Jenn Granneman's *Introvert, Dear* website, there's an article by Effie Ochago titled *Why Introverts Should Stay Physically Active.* Ochago does a terrific job explaining the benefits of exercise for introverts. Among the reasons she mentions are stress reduction, calming an overthinking mind, and reducing anxiety.

No wonder I was able to hold myself together at my new job. At least until my back gave out.

Exercise can be your best friend. It doesn't have to be the martial arts. Do whatever works for you. Weightlifting, boxing, running, hiking, swimming, roller skating, and even a simple daily walk. The important thing is that it's something you enjoy ean do consistently.

Of course, always check with your doctor first before beginning any exercise program.

There's a lot of advice out there on how introverts can use this strategy or that strategy to get by in an extroverted world. But if you exercise regularly, that's a cheat code that checks off many of the boxes. It'll keep you fully recharged and ahead of the curve.

PICK YOU

In the *Don't Pop the Bubble* chapter, I recommended being careful about letting people know what you're up to. Other people may distract you with their own ideas and suggestions.

There's nothing inherently wrong with ideas and suggestions. They have their place. For example, during a brainstorming session. But when you're locked in? That's when it's time to lock others out.

At face value, this sounds like terrible advice.

Don't listen to what anyone says! You're a genius and everyone else is an idiot!

It's less about well-meaning people and any helpful feedback they may have. It's more about how your mind works as an introvert.

In a nutshell: the ideas and suggestions that can inspire you in the beginning can also keep you from finishing what you started.

We think and we overthink. We get in our own way. It's who we are. Once we finally get started on whatever we're working on, it's best to tune everything out from that point forward. It's not that we need to protect ourselves from other people. We need to protect ourselves from ourselves.

The less clutter bouncing around in our minds, the better.

But what if you get stuck? What if you reach a point where you're not sure where you're going and actually need some help?

Enter PickFu.

I discovered PickFu when I had trouble choosing a title for this book. I was stuck between *People Suck* and a safer, more professional-sounding option. As always, I overanalyzed everything. I needed something that could help me arrive at a decision without any further mental gymnastics.

I did an Internet search on how to choose a title. Next thing you know, I was directed to PickFu. It's a consumer research platform that does surveys and other stuff that helps you get honest feedback. It can help you decide on a title, cover design, and much more.

For those of you who overthink like I do, this is a godsend.

First and foremost, this is not like informally asking for feedback on social media. Any feedback you get on social media is likely skewed thanks to bias from your family, friends, and yes, even people who don't like you.

With PickFu, you get to do surveys that involve 50 to 500 random people. These are people who don't know you, aren't biased in favor of or against you, and aren't going to bother you with follow-up questions or unsolicited advice. You do the survey, you get the data, and you're done.

Now this is how an introvert wants to do business.

I used PickFu to make a final decision on whether or not to go with *People Suck*. Obviously, *People Suck* won. And everyone at Pick-Fu was great.

But it went beyond just helping me choose a title. It helped empower me. Because when you use a platform like PickFu, you get a fascinating, up-close look at human nature.

The first part of the survey was a tallied-up vote. If you want to go with an entirely statistics-based approach, X amount of people voted for *People Suck* and Y amount of people voted for the other option. X was greater than Y. Statistically speaking, that was the ballgame right there.

But wait! It got more interesting than that.

Under the official vote, there's a section where people in the survey get to share their feedback.

I was impressed.

These people did not give vanilla answers such as *I liked it* or *People Suck sucks*. The respondents took the time to give genuine, specific feedback. I truly appreciate the effort they put into it.

The fascinating part? They all said things that contradicted each other, yet somehow none of them were wrong.

One person said that *People Suck* was not professional and that the other title was. I can tell you without a doubt that this feedback was spot on.

Another person contradicted that. This person said that the other title was too boring, while *People Suck* made them laugh and want to know more. Again, spot on.

As I read through all of the comments, I could see there were plenty of people who loved Option A and didn't like Option B, and vice versa. Some of them were a bit salty in their disapproval of a title. One person hated both. All of them backed up their opinions with solid reasons why.

That's when it hit me:

No matter what you do, someone's going to love it and someone's going to hate it. So why sweat it?

Once this truth sinks in, you're free. You're no longer worried about trying to make everyone happy because you know it's impossible. PickFu mathematically proved that. Might as well let it go. No need to fuss. You can just be you. How awesome is that?

DEAFTROVERT

Susan Cain's *Quiet* is the first introvert-related book I've ever read. It grabbed me by the collar. It said *Hey! There's nothing wrong with you. You've been bending over backward trying to accommodate people who are different than you.* I was particularly fond of the anecdotes involving Professor Brian Little. His need to get into a quiet zone to mentally prepare for a presentation is exactly how I roll.

Soon afterward, I found several other introvert authors covering similar topics. Each and every one of them is a valuable resource. To read their works is validating.

As introverts, we often question ourselves. This is usually influenced by well-meaning extroverts who genuinely wonder why we don't always show up for happy hour.

"What? You can't come to the party? But everyone will be there! Cindy's in town and she's really looking forward to seeing you!"

We get bombarded with negative messages if we don't behave the way our more outgoing friends and relatives expect. Sometimes, these messages get in our head.

Don't like to go out much? *You're antisocial.*

Don't like small talk? *You lack conversation skills.*

Highly sensitive? *You're too emotional.*

Tend to be quiet and reserved? *You're too shy.*

Can't think of what to say when asked a question? *You're too slow.*

If you're not careful, you start believing it. You feel obligated to slip into people-pleasing mode and set yourself up for yet another introvert hangover. For our own well-being, we need to know when and where to draw the line.

First, set boundaries. If you're exhausted after a long week at work, claim Friday evenings as your own personal recharge time. Or maybe you're fine with taking a quick nap early Friday evening, and then going out later. If you're more of a Saturday person, go out on Saturday then. Maybe you prefer just one or two Saturdays a month. Maybe you prefer not going out at all. Or maybe you do like going out regularly, but only in smaller groups. Perhaps you'd rather go to a museum instead of a nightclub.

None of the above options are wrong. Whatever works, you gotta do you.

Second, we need to reframe ourselves.

Don't like to go out much? *You're independent.*

Don't like small talk? *You're into deep conversation.*

Highly sensitive? *You're empathetic and a good friend.*

Tend to be quiet and reserved? *You're a good listener.*

Can't think of what to say when asked a question? *You rely on long-term memory, and it's a veritable smorgasbord of creativity when it's unlocked.*

All of the aforementioned reading resources (you'll find them in the recommended reading section at the end of this book) brought forth a new level of self-awareness. And as all of this new self-awareness unfolded, a nagging sense of déjà vu persisted.

It turns out that I've already written about this from a different angle. A deaf angle. *Deaf Again, Anything But Silent, Madness in the*

Mainstream, and *That Deaf Kid.* There's definitely a parallel between the deaf world and the introvert world. It's a journey of self-discovery where you look everywhere for answers to a problem, only to find out there was nothing you needed to fix.

You're not broken. It's other people's perspectives that happen to be warped.

As mentioned in the *Mental Gymnastics* chapter, there used to be a time when I would actually apologize for being deaf. I'd buy something at the store and whenever the cashier asked me a question, I couldn't help myself.

"Huh? Whazzat? I'm sorry, I can't hear."

The funny thing is that more often than not, when I apologized for who I was, it elicited a negative response. It could be an eye roll, a sigh, or a terse response that made me feel like *how dare I waste this person's time.*

These days, if anyone shows a hint of exasperation because I'm deaf, I respond in American Sign Language.

"Hey, waitaminute. I'm deaf. I sign ASL. What's up with those breakfast sandwiches? I thought the ad said two for the price of one."

More often than not, most cashiers realize right away what's going on. At which point *they* apologize and immediately adapt by gesturing or using pen and paper. Some of the cashiers, after regular interaction, gradually pick up ASL. I love it. When I'm unapologetically deaf, it earns respect.

Introverts can do the same.

Here's a powerful quote by E.E. Cummings:

The hardest fight a man has to fight is to live in a world where every single day someone is trying to make you someone you do not want to be.

Why should living your life be a fight? Let go and be your damn fine self.

It helps immensely when you learn that there are others like you. At Gallaudet University, the world's only university for deaf and hard of hearing students, you can see this happening every year at freshman orientation. A lot of incoming students come from mainstream schools where they never had an opportunity to meet another deaf person. You can see their jaws drop when they set foot on the Gallaudet campus for the first time.

"Oh my god. I thought I was the only one."

I've felt the same way when I've read the works of other introverts.

Another parallel between deaf people and introverts is our visibility (or lack thereof). Deafness has often been described as an invisible disability. It's true. Countless times, people have given me an attitude because they thought I was ignoring them. Unless I'm wearing neon-colored hearing aids or visibly communicating in sign language, no one can see that I'm deaf.

Likewise, you can't see an introvert. You might think you know what an introvert looks like, but there's no actual "look." It's not always a quiet person sitting alone in a corner.

If you think that's the definition of an introvert, Michael Jordan would like a word with you. As would Chris Rock, Amy Schumer, Oprah Winfrey, and many other introverts who have entertained millions of fans.

Another similarity is a special talent that deaf people and introverts have developed out of necessity. We've mastered the art of social bluffing. Deaf people often pretend to understand what people say by constantly nodding their heads. Introverts often show up at events and pretend to enjoy them, all the while wishing they were relaxing back home with a good book.

It needs to be pointed out that social bluffing does not indicate total dissatisfaction. A deaf person can enjoy the company of one person while struggling to understand another. An introvert may enjoy a social event at the outset, only to later feel a desire to leave after their energy level has subsided.

In each scenario, we have people spending time outside of their comfort zone. More often than not, they feel a sense of obligation to do so.

In *Deaf Again*, there's an anecdote about a 12-year-old deaf kid who practices social bluffing at family events. As the only deaf person in his family, he methodically works the room. He feels it's his responsibility to connect with others. Sooner or later, he gets exhausted. He politely greets everyone and maintains a facade as long as he can before retreating to his room to play video games. This is a classic *deaf recharge*.

When deaf people work hard to understand what others are saying, it sets off a mentally and physically draining reaction that's known as *concentration fatigue*. It's a close cousin of the introvert hangover. Deaf writer Ian Noon said it best with an article titled *The Impact of Concentration Fatigue on Deaf Children Should be Factored In*.

"I went to a great conference today," Noon says at the beginning of the article. *"It was riveting and I was hooked on pretty much every word. And then I got home and collapsed on the sofa. I'm not just tired, I'm shattered."*

Sound familiar?

That's right. It's the deaf version of Jenn Granneman's *12 Signs You Have an 'Introvert Hangover' (Yes, It's Real)*.

Not everything about the deaf and introvert communities match. One minor difference is the *dominate a conversation* social bluffing strategy that some deaf people have been known to use. There are times when a deaf person might take a deep breath, start talking, and never stop.

The whole point of this tactic is simple: *the more I talk, the less chance I'll misunderstand anything you say—because I'm not letting you say anything at all*. How brilliant is that? But it's exhausting, and you won't find many introverts dominating a conversation.

Perhaps the biggest discrepancy can be found in advocacy. I feel way more empowered as a deaf person than as an introvert. We have the Americans with Disabilities Act. We have captioned TV and captioned movies. We have sign language interpreters readily available to bridge the communication gap between the hearing and the deaf.

We have hearing people connecting with the deaf on a deeper level by learning sign language. There's a wide range of assistive devices at our disposal. Bottom line: if I advocate for myself as a deaf person, people believe me.

As an introvert? Not so much.

"You missed an awesome party last night, Drolz. You're getting old.

DOUBLE TROUBLE

In my book *Madness in the Mainstream,* one of the chapters details a seventh-grade camping trip. I was a new student at a large school where there were over 100 students in my grade. The camping trip was an annual event that takes place right before the beginning of the school year. It's meant to ensure a smooth transition from elementary school to middle school. It's believed that team-building activities, in a relaxing environment away from home, is a great way to get the school year off to a good start.

Unfortunately, if you're the only deaf kid in your school, there's no such thing as a relaxing environment. As both a deaf kid and an introvert, this weekend trip had "disaster" written all over it. As a 13-year-old, I had no understanding of this.

When I was dropped off at the school parking lot, I was overwhelmed by the sheer number of students milling around. I came from an elementary school where there were only 12 people in my grade. I was now amongst almost ten times more people. Right off the bat, I was lost.

There were maybe four or five kids I knew from little league. I swapped a quick how-do-ya-do with each of them. Sure, I could play with them for two hours on a baseball field, but a two-hour bus ride was another story. I didn't say another word to anyone as I sat silently by the window.

As the buses arrived at the campgrounds, I grabbed my stuff and played the old game of *figure out where the hell I'm going.* As various staff announced who needed to go where for what activity, I had to corner them afterward to remind them I'm deaf.

In some mainstream programs this is lauded as "having excellent self-advocacy skills." Yeah, right. My anxiety level was off the charts.

Soon I figured out which group I was assigned to and followed what they were doing the best that I could. I could not understand a word anyone said.

Time to go into survival mode.

During the team-building activities, I got into the habit of making sure I stayed near the end of the line. This way I was able to buy enough time to figure out what we were doing. By the time it was my turn, it looked like I was an old pro. Some of the staff actually thought I was able to follow their directives. Until...

"Mark, stay off the asphalt."

As we walked down the road toward the next team-building activity, our staff leader wanted to make sure we stayed off to the side in case there was any oncoming traffic. It took me a while to figure this out.

"Huh?"

Was he talking to me?

"Mark, I said stay off the asphalt."

Shit. He's definitely talking to me. And everyone's staring.

"Huh?"

This was embarrassing. Could it possibly get any worse?

Yes, it could.

One of those kids who played in my rec baseball league realized what was going on. He moved closer to me so I could read his lips.

"He said stay off the asphalt."

"Huh? Wave off my ass fart?"

Welcome to junior high, kid.

Later that evening, the whole seventh grade gathered together in a large cabin. A staff leader barked out directions, and once again I just stood there without a clue while several students broke off into smaller groups. They huddled in circles and appeared to be planning something. Was it some kind of competition? A scavenger hunt? Ghost stories? Who knew?

As far as I could tell, whatever activity was going on must have been an optional one. Some of the students stayed seated where they were. I moved toward the back of the room and sat behind them.

I had no idea at the time, but as a budding introvert I would learn that the back of the room was my safe space. At least if people left me alone while I was there.

One by one, each group took turns performing an improvisational skit. I sat there bored out of my mind. Time slowed down to an agonizing eternity.

Uh-oh. The staff leader is looking at me again. What does he want now?

Apparently, the skits were pretty good and the staff decided everyone should get involved. I could see the staff leader pointing toward kids in the back and calling them out. My heart skipped a beat when he briefly made eye contact with me. As discreetly as possible, I moved to the other side of the room. Damned if I was going to let him put me in a position where I'd make a total ass out of myself.

There had to be a way out of this mess. I glanced around in desperation and found the exit. Standing in front of the door—and my escape from Hearing People Hell—was another staff leader. It was Caroline, my soon-to-be history teacher. I'd managed to establish a friendly rapport with her earlier in the day. Perhaps if I talked to her, she'd understand.

"Uh, Caroline?" I stammered.

"Yes, Mark?"

"I twisted my ankle today and it's really bothering me. Mind if I go back to the campground and lie down?"

Was that a lame-ass excuse or what?

At first, Caroline glanced across the room, perhaps looking for whoever had the first aid kit. It would only take a couple of minutes to wrap my allegedly sore ankle. But then Caroline stopped and looked me in the eye.

"Are you sure?"

Caroline wasn't stupid. She knew exactly what was going on. She saw that I was *done.*

"Yeah. I just need to rest up. I'll be fine."

Again, without being aware that I was an introvert on top of being the only deaf kid in my school, I had no idea that I was instinctively seeking an opportunity to recharge.

"Okay, go ahead. Good night, Mark."

I thanked Caroline and headed back to the campground, where I curled up in my sleeping bag and gazed at the stars.

I breathed a sigh of relief. The stars were much better company than anyone in the cabin. At that moment I might have been alone, but at least I was no longer lonely. That's just the way it is.

This was a huge turning point in my life. It was right there in that sleeping bag, lying alone under the stars, when I realized that I was on my own. As long as I allowed other people to make decisions for me, my life was going to be a living hell. This was the start of a long process where I would gradually learn how to advocate for myself.

It was also the start of a long process where I would learn that it's much easier to advocate for myself as a deaf person than as an introvert. As a deaf person, I had it figured out in my twenties. As an introvert, it would take a few decades longer.

And here's the rub:

You can't advocate for something without any awareness of it.

In the *Wipeout on a New Wave* chapter, my thrill of meeting other deaf kids was offset by my inability to understand myself as an introvert.

When I became a student at Gallaudet University, I was better prepared. I was older and wiser. I was more aware of my comfort zone and chose to hang out in smaller groups. I was able to make new friends much faster. Attending classes with other deaf students offered plenty of topics for conversation. Being an introvert did not slow me down. In fact, without realizing it, I naturally gravitated toward other introverts who had a lot in common with me. As a result, there were no barriers blocking my ability to understand myself as a deaf person.

When a deaf person is surrounded by other deaf people, including successful deaf role models, a self-imposed glass ceiling completely shatters. You learn that it's okay to be exactly who you are.

As an introvert? Eh. That would take a bit longer to figure out.

And now the $100,000 question:

When do introverts, in a society that perpetually rewards extroverted behaviors, get to learn it's okay to be exactly who they are?

OVERTHINKING AND PEOPLE-PLEASING

Overthinking, which introverts tend to do, is like a mental rain delay.

Should I do this, should I do that, what about this, what about that…

Stop. Take a deep breath. Mentally envision an eject button catapulting all of the clutter out of your mind. Just pause, take a moment to understand what's happening, and then regroup.

When we overthink, we allow ourselves to be consumed by external forces. We worry that we're going to mess up and look stupid. And the reason we worry that we're going to mess up and look stupid is because we worry about what other people think.

Note: the kind of overthinking I speak of is the kind that slows us down. Worrying, self-doubt, and fear of failure. This is not to be confused with being deliberate, fact-checking, and allowing our long-term memory to do its job before we speak up. The former is a barrier. The latter is a strength.

All of us, to some extent, want to gain someone else's approval. It's an ego boost. But if you rely on this for your own sense of well-being, it's a trap you don't want to fall into.

When you worry about what other people think, you lean on them. Fail at something, and you fall flat on your face.

When you don't worry about what other people think, you stand on your own two feet. You're balanced. Fail at something, and you're still standing. It's not even a failure. It's a learning experience. You've gained information that will help you do better next time.

Worrying about what other people think also leads to another bad habit: people-pleasing. People-pleasing is not to be confused with being a kind person.

How can you be a kind person if you're being fake? You're not even being kind to yourself.

Andrew Leedham, in his book *Unstoppable Self Confidence*, made a sobering point: if you're constantly people-pleasing and approval seeking, eventually you lose track of who you are. You're so busy seeking external approval and validation that you forget *you*.

Hey! Where have we seen this before?

It's like Leedham and I live in parallel worlds.

In my books *Madness in the Mainstream* and *That Deaf Kid*, there's information about how deaf and hard of hearing people are programmed by introjects.

Introjection happens when we unconsciously absorb the thoughts, beliefs, attitudes, and behaviors of the people around us. When our parents, teachers, and members of society at large directly or indirectly impose any *you shoulds* on us, we internalize it.

Introjects don't have to be verbal. Kids watch their parents' actions and internalize just about anything. It creates a cycle that's hard to break. If we have enough self-awareness, the day eventually arrives when we look in the mirror and say *"omigod! I'm behaving just like my parents!"*

Introjects block people from being their genuine selves. This includes deaf and hard of hearing people who people-please their way through mainstream society without embracing their own deaf identity.

With deaf and hard of hearing children, especially those in mainstream schools, there are introjects that make them believe it's their responsibility to assimilate into the hearing world, often at the expense of their own happiness.

For example, deaf and hard of hearing children are constantly reminded to *sit up front, pay attention, wear your hearing aids, read my lips*, and so on. They're frequently reminded that they don't participate in class discussion enough, as if it's their fault they couldn't understand what anyone said.

As a result, thousands of deaf and hard of hearing children resort to Mainstream Survival Skills. They go out of their way to use clever strategies that make it look like they're fitting in. They fake it until they make it. They try their best to do what their hearing parents and teachers want. They're people-pleasing.

But when they get a chance to meet other deaf and hard of hearing peers, they eventually learn that they can succeed in life on their own terms. They learn to use strategies that actually work for them, not strategies that merely give the appearance of fitting in.

This is the beauty of peers and role models: when you meet another person *just like you* who has it all figured out, it opens a new world of opportunity.

It doesn't matter who you are. I don't care if you're hearing, deaf, hard of hearing, introverted, or extroverted. This is a truth that applies to all of us.

Don't fall for the many *you shoulds* that stifle your authentic self. Look inward for who you really are. If you're deaf, be deaf. If you're an introvert, be an introvert.

If this is one of those *easier said than done* things for you—and for many of us it is—grab a copy of Leedham's *Unstoppable Self Confidence*. It'll clear those *you shoulds* out of your mind. Go for it. Your authentic self is worth it.

OVERTHINKING WITH LOVE

Wawa, Inc., has a chain of convenience stores all over the East Coast. They make the best coffee. I stop by my local Wawa all the time and wind up getting more than just coffee.

My wife often reminds me how this siphons money out of my wallet. She's right, but the coffee is *so damn good* and you can't help grabbing something else while you're there.

Soon after my family moved to a neighboring town, I promised Melanie I'd be more frugal. I brewed my own coffee at home and cut down on my daily excursions to Wawa. For once, I was being fiscally responsible.

Yeah, right.

There was a Wawa less than a mile from our new home.

Must. Resist. The. Urge.

A month later, my family returned from an out-of-state softball tournament. We were too tired for a regular meal. We agreed to stop at the new Wawa and order some sandwiches to go.

We went into this Wawa—the one I promised I would avoid as much as possible—and got everything we needed. As we placed the items on the counter, the cashier rang them up and put them in a bag. At which point she smiled at me and signed "thank you" in ASL. Another cashier emerged from the back office and promptly waved hello.

Busted.

"Come here often?" Melanie asked, with a wry grin.

"Just once in a while," I shrugged.

Eventually, I found a healthy balance between good coffee and wise spending. Nowadays, I only go to Wawa in the mornings for a cup of coffee and maybe a breakfast sandwich. Or two.

There's a different Wawa on my route to work so I got into the habit of stopping by at that one instead. As always, I use ASL when communicating with the staff.

If you sign regularly amongst hearing people, they wind up doing it, too.

A short time later, the pandemic hit. Things got thrown out of whack.

When things slowly returned to normal, I continued stopping by at this Wawa. For a while there, face masks were mandatory. Lip-reading was obviously not going to work. It didn't matter. The staff consistently used a combination of gesturing and basic sign language to communicate with me.

There was one cashier who worked the morning shift full time. I saw her every day. She wrapped up every transaction with a signed "thank you." A simple gesture, but it meant a lot to me.

Warning: Just because something is simple doesn't mean nothing can go wrong. There's plenty that can go wrong with ASL if you don't master the nuances. For example, that simple "thank you" only requires bringing an open palm to your chin and then softly lowering it. But if you inadvertently put that open palm a little further under your chin, that "thank you" becomes "eff you." It has happened.

Finally, they lifted the mask mandate. For the first time in two years, I could see my favorite cashier's face. I smiled as I purchased my daily cup of coffee. She smiled back. I signed "thank you."

She lifted her open palm to her lips, lowered it, and blew a kiss.

Omigod. Like I said, there's plenty that can go wrong.

I froze.

Eh. Maybe it was just a mistake.

I returned the next day.

It was not a mistake.

For the second day in a row, the cashier ended the transaction by blowing a kiss.

She's been blowing me kisses under that mask for two years! Who knew?

This is where the overthinking hit me.

How could I not notice she blew kisses for two years? Okay, she had a mask on, but still, were there other cues I might have missed? Hand placement? Body language? A twinkle in her eye? How am I going to explain *this* to Melanie the next time we go in the store together?

I went back the next day.

Smooch. Mwah!

More overthinking.

I know. In the last chapter, I said we need to stop overthinking. Yet here I was in a convenience store doing it again. Old habits are hard to break. Besides, this situation caught me completely off guard. We had a cashier blowing me kisses on a daily basis. All I could think was "how am I supposed to correct this?"

The cashier was clearly not flirting or anything of the sort. She was merely repeating what she thought she saw me do when I signed "thank you" with a mask covering my face. She must have assumed there was a mutual *mwah* going on. Perhaps she thought it was a societal norm in deaf culture.

My overthinking kicked into overdrive.

If I correct her mistake, the mistake that I allowed to go on for two years, she's going to be embarrassed. The mere mention of a kiss makes everything awkward. She'll never look me in the eye again. Or maybe she thought I actually was flirting from the get-go and she responded in kind? That would be even more awkward. Ugh. Maybe I should say nothing. But wait! What if I say nothing, and then someone else corrects her? She'd be pissed off. There are other deaf customers who frequent that store. How could I allow her to unknowingly blow kisses at every Tom, Dick, and Harry?

Once again, my thought process was off the rails.

Say something, Drolz!

Finally, I had an idea.

I returned to the store the next day for my daily cup of java.

Smooch. Mwah!

"Call me," I responded seductively.

Of course I didn't do that. This is my favorite cashier at my favorite store.

But seriously, I simply didn't have the nerve to say "that's a kiss. Move your palm a little lower and eliminate the smooch. There you go."

Who knows, maybe an extrovert would've had no problem saying that. But I'm an overthinking introvert, so here's how I subtly handled it:

The following day, and each day forward, I consistently modeled the correct behavior. Without a mask blocking my mouth, I signed "thank you" and enunciated the words with my lips. She caught on and adjusted accordingly.

Hearing people can read lips, too. Who'da thunk it?

A platonic relationship remains intact, Melanie isn't mad at me, and I still get the best coffee in the world.

HIGHLY SENSITIVE

At one of my *Madness in the Mainstream* presentations, I got into the part that explains how deaf students in mainstream schools go to great lengths to look like they're fitting in, even when they have no clue what anyone else is saying.

I mentioned my son Brandon. Brandon isn't deaf, but thanks to his older brother Darren—who is deaf—Brandon knows all about the infamous *Mainstream Survival Skills of the Deaf and Hard of Hearing*. He can see it from a mile away. He was all of ten years old when he came home and told us there was another deaf kid at his school.

We had no idea. We thought it was just Darren and one other kid. No one ever mentioned a third deaf student.

This other deaf kid flew under the radar because he didn't use sign language. It didn't matter. Brandon still knew. This mystery kid, whoever he was, used the exact same social bluffing techniques that Darren got away with many times before.

There are deaf kids who try to act like they can hear because they're embarrassed about being deaf. Some of them are even coached to act that way. They're told it's their responsibility to work on their listening and speaking skills because it's a hearing world. But just like introverts who feel obliged to behave like extroverts, it's not a genuine way to go about your life.

For whatever reason, this student was never given a chance to interact with Darren, who was only one year older and would have been an awesome role model.

I repeated my infamous joke that the two kids had to be kept apart because the school district didn't want any cross-contamination.

Watch out! You'll catch his deaf! You'll start talking with your hands or something!

The audience laughed at the cross-contamination joke. Except for one person all the way in the back row. I saw it clear as day. In an auditorium packed with 200 people, I easily noticed the one person whose affect had completely changed.

It was a woman in her thirties. Out of all the people smiling, I saw her expression go from *relaxed smile* to *clearly bothered.*

It could have been anything. Maybe she suddenly realized she left her phone at home. Maybe the person sitting next to her farted. But she was definitely the one person in the building who was not a happy camper.

Let it go, Drolz. There are 199 people having a good time. Don't let one person get in your head. You can't make them all happy.

She got in my head. I went on with the presentation and all went well, but I kept mentally checking in on her to make sure she was okay.

All right, she doesn't look as alarmed as she did five minutes ago. I wonder if she's a parent of a deaf child. Maybe I hit a nerve. Maybe what happened at my kids' school happened to someone she knew. Hey! What if that was HER kid?

There was another anecdote I wanted to share about the hardships deaf kids face in the mainstream, but I decided to skip over it. I didn't want to risk further upsetting the person in the back row.

There are times when I see people in the audience with defensive body language. That's fine. People can disagree with me all they want. But if I've upset someone? That's different. I'm too much of an empath. It feels like there's been a disturbance in the force.

I moved on to the *so what are we gonna do about it* segment of the presentation. It wraps up with an inspirational message. Toward the end, I glanced up at the back row.

She was smiling again. Whew. I felt better. Balance had been restored.

I'm always telling people not to worry about what others think. Introverts have a habit of being people pleasers. We have to remind ourselves we can't make all of the people happy all of the time. It's not our job. Yet somehow, it's a hard habit to break.

I believe part of it comes from the fact that introverts wear a figurative mask when we step out of our comfort zone. Sometimes we deviate from who we are when we go out and do extrovert things with our extrovert friends. The danger of wearing a mask is we may lose touch with our authentic selves. We try so hard to fit in with others that we forget our own needs. And then *boom*, we have an introvert hangover.

But there's more to it than that. I'm mindful not to be a people pleaser anymore. I wasn't people-pleasing that night when one person in the audience looked out of sorts. It was something else, and it was something I had intentionally ignored for a long time.

I'm highly sensitive.

There are articles everywhere about highly sensitive people. But each time I saw the words *highly sensitive*, my eyes would glaze over it. I genuinely believed it didn't apply to me.

I'm a guy. I'm not supposed to be sensitive. Go ahead and disagree with me, but that's the message society sends.

There's a friend of mine, Manny, who doesn't look anything like a highly sensitive person. But he is. He lamented about it over drinks one night.

"I don't get it," Manny said. "I was dating this woman who told me she loves guys who are open with their feelings. She said she wants a guy who's not afraid to be vulnerable. Being vulnerable is a sign of strength. At least that's what she said."

"What happened?" I asked.

"I opened up. I admitted there's some stuff I'm worried about."

"How'd that go?"

"She friend-zoned me. Haven't heard from her in a week."

"Manny," I shook my head. "Suck it up and take your blood pressure meds like a man."

We laughed, but we knew the stereotype was for real.

In *The Irresistable Introvert,* Michaela Chung correctly points out that our sensitivity is seen as a weakness. It shouldn't be, but it is. Chung's comment applies to everyone regardless of gender, but for people like Manny—and me—it feels amplified for men. And this is precisely why every time I'd seen the words *highly sensitive* in an article, I'd skip over it. Even if the title somehow resonated.

Again, I'm a guy. I can't possibly be highly sensitive.

Next thing you know, I'm pacing the floor of a college auditorium, simultaneously delivering a kick-ass presentation and mentally processing *50 Ways I May Have Upset That Person in The Back Row.*

Enough's enough. What's the deal with this highly sensitive stuff? I had to know.

It didn't take long to find an answer. There's a great website dedicated to the topic. Check out *Highly Sensitive Refuge* (highlysensitiverefuge.com). It's an online community for highly sensitive people created by Jenn Granneman and Andre Sólo.

Yes, the same Jenn Granneman behind the wildly popular Introvert, Dear *website. She also writes about highly sensitive people and it's as spot on as her writings about introverts.*

Two things immediately stood out: first, if you're highly sensitive, there's nothing wrong with you. It's considered a normal trait. And that's the second thing: it's actually a genetic trait.

The characteristics of introverts and highly sensitive people often overlap. They're similar enough that people might assume highly sensitive people are a subgroup of introverts. This is not the case. In Granneman's article titled *21 Signs That You're a Highly Sensitive Person,* she points out that 30% of highly sensitive people are actually extroverts.

As I read through the *21 Signs* article, my jaw dropped to the floor. *Why didn't I pay attention to any of this before?*

I forwarded the article to my wife, Melanie. She needed to see there's a reason behind some of my behaviors. Among them:

Abruptly changing the channel when there's a violent or gory scene on TV. It doesn't matter if it's the eleven o'clock news or a fictional scene in a medical drama such as *Grey's Anatomy.* I can't watch that stuff. I literally feel it—even for a fictional character—and my empathy overwhelms me. You can usually find me watching comedy or science fiction because those genres are an escape. "There's enough drama in real life," I told Melanie. "Why would I want to watch more of it on TV?"

Emotional exhaustion—from other peoples' feelings. That person in the back row actually drained some of my mental energy. And that was nothing compared to what goes on at home. I can easily sense when my wife, kids, and even the pets are upset about something. I can't function until I know they're okay. Oh, and by the way, I'm also a school counselor. *Burnout, anyone?*

Time pressure. The clock always gets to me. Yes, I'm always on time at work. But deadlines overstimulate me, as does tardiness. If my kids are late for school and I have to drop them off, they're calm as a cucumber while I'm an emotional wreck. They never get sent to detention hall because the principal knows I've already punished myself.

Being jumpy and easily startled. I have a hypersensitive startle reflex. Tap me on the shoulder while I'm working on a book. Go ahead, it's amusing. It usually results in a loud scream followed by me swinging from the chandelier.

There's more, but instead I encourage you to head over to highlysensitiverefuge.com for the full scoop. The only thing I want to add is that although the above examples may give the impression that highly sensitive people are a hot mess, the fact remains that our traits—as with introverts—can be a source of strength. The same mental energy that caused me to overthink that person in the back row can also lead to a new book, a new community support program, a new art project, and so on.

Regardless of whether you're an introvert or a highly sensitive person—or both—your inner dialogue can be a source of tremendous creativity.

I DON'T CARE

Anne and Matt's wedding was scheduled to take place in April of 2020. Every little detail was meticulously planned a year in advance.

Then COVID-19 hit.

It was initially thought that with the proper measures in place, the pandemic would fade away in a few weeks. Just to be sure, the wedding was rescheduled almost a year later.

Oops.

Another postponement. It would be more than two years before Anne and Matt finally tied the knot. They made it worth the wait.

This was the first public event my family attended since the pandemic began. Everyone had been vaccinated, and we felt safe enough to party with people like we used to.

It was the lull in the storm before the pandemic struck back with the Omicron variant. But for the time being, this was the closest return to normal we had.

The wedding took place outdoors, in a beautiful garden adjacent to a private banquet hall. The place was all ours and it was time to party.

It was one of the most beautiful weddings we'd ever seen. It was a celebration of Anne and Matt's love, commitment, and resilience. Soon after Anne and Matt exchanged their vows, we heard the three words we waited a long time to hear them say:

"Open bar, everyone!"

Alcohol flowed freely as the DJ rocked the house with one hit song after the other.

Everyone dances at weddings, but this was different. This was two years' worth of pent-up energy.

People only sat down for the customary dinner, toast, and cake. Other than that, everyone was either on the dance floor or at the bar.

I noticed Anne cutting a rug with the bridesmaids. Nice, but...

"Where's Matt?" I asked.

"Outside," said one of my kids. "He's hammered."

"How do you know?"

"I joined him. I'm hammered, too."

Matt came back and reunited with Anne on the dance floor.

Yes, he was hammered. As were the groomsmen.

It was like *The Hangover*. All we needed was Ken Jeong jumping out of the trunk of our car.

About an hour later, one of my kids (no, I'm not naming names—what happens in Philly, stays in Philly) tapped me on the shoulder.

"You're not gonna believe what I saw in the bathroom," he said.

"Matt passed out?"

"Nah. He's still going strong. But one of the groomsmen is changing into a catsuit."

"You have got to be kiddin—oh my god."

There was this huge guy, about six foot three, wearing a super-tight catsuit and twerking on the dance floor. Everyone cheered him on.

That's when the realization struck me that Mr. Catsuit looked *exactly* like my daughter's softball coach. I called my daughter over.

"How about that," I said, pointing at the sweaty guy grinding on the floor. "Doesn't he kind of look like Coach Harvey?"

"Oh my god! Dad! I can't unsee that!"

Coach Harvey, if you're reading this, I have pictures.

It got worse. Mr. Catsuit dropped on his back and lifted his legs, thrusting them up and down in sync with the music. It looked like the mating call of a hot and bothered panther.

The mating call worked. Several other partygoers joined Mr. Catsuit. It was total bedlam.

At that moment, I sensed a presence behind me and turned around. It was a 75-year-old man holding a glass of champagne. He looked blissfully serene amidst the hell breaking loose around him.

It was Harold. Anne's dad.

"I don't care," he said, with a big grin as he patted me on the back.

We gave each other a knowing glance and directed our eyes back to the dance floor.

Mr. Catsuit was humping someone's leg.

"I don't care," Harold repeated. His face beamed with joy.

I understood. It's a special moment that has stuck with me to this day.

Harold had applied *I don't care* in the most powerful way imaginable. He did not judge. He did not deny what was going on around him. He simply knew that this was the most special day in his and his daughter's life, and nothing else mattered. He genuinely did not care. Instead, he was genuinely happy. There's power in letting go of the small things and appreciating what's really important.

For the record, the rest of us didn't care, either. We had a fantastic time. If you wanted to go streaking in the parking lot, it would have been fine. We didn't care.

This is probably the most off-the-point anecdote in the whole book. *I don't care. We're rolling with this.*

There are two types of *I don't care* that I've seen. The first one is the *I don't care* of a person who has given up. I've seen students with a Bluto Blutarsky grade point average shrug and say *I don't care* as everything in their lives fell apart. This is the *I don't care* of someone who is overwhelmed, unsure of what to do, and feeling hopeless. That's the kind of *I don't care* that we want to work our way out of, hopefully with the right kind of support.

But Harold's *I don't care*? That was the *I don't care* of a person letting go. A release. It frees you from the shackles of *you should do this, you should do that.* It's thumbing your nose at conformity. Carpe diem.

If you're an introvert, letting go of what others think is the first step to healthy self-awareness. Instead of being overly concerned about societal norms, how about just being yourself? Make a bowl of popcorn. Watch that movie you recorded. Alone or with a friend.

I don't care.

You don't have to, either.

SATISFACTION

There are plenty of introvert-related books and articles out there. I enjoy reading them. They're empowering. Browse through them, and you'll find people who have much in common with you.

Sometimes, another introvert makes you realize there's a better way of doing things. A way that's aligned with your strengths. On rare occasions, you'll find one who connects with a mind-blowing paradigm shift.

In Benjamin Plumb's *The Satisfied Introvert: A Memoir About Finding Safety in an Extroverted World*, that's precisely what happened. A nice, fascinating read suddenly morphed into... *omigod! I can't believe I missed that!*

Early in his book, Plumb shares an anecdote about a grade school assignment. He had to choose a current event and present it to his class. To overcome the trepidation that came with this assignment, he rehearsed multiple times over multiple days. It worked.

At first glance, I saw nothing wrong with this. It resonated because it's exactly what I do before any public speaking event. I rehearse. Repeatedly. Over and over, until the cows come home. Sometimes my wife intervenes and tells me it's time to stop. But I've always believed that overpreparing is a good thing. It helps me overcome my inconsistent ability to call upon my short-term memory, and it gives me the confidence to be on stage in front of a large audience.

But there's a catch. I'll come back to that in a bit.

Plumb describes himself as *methodical* in his approach at school and at work. Again, I saw nothing wrong with it. There are times when this approach can bring forth good results.

For example, at the Pennsylvania School for the Deaf, I was tasked with compiling a report that would help my counseling team become a Recognized ASCA Model Program under the American School Counselor Association.

I love writing. When I was asked to collect data and write reports for our RAMP application, of course I jumped at the opportunity.

One problem: I have the attention span of a flea.

I got easily distracted. My office was in a location where there was heavy traffic and a lot of people stopped by to say hello. Each time this happened, I lost track of what I was doing. I was in a constant state of stopping and starting without actually getting anywhere.

My closest colleagues noticed this and came up with a brilliant solution.

They put me in the basement.

No joke. It was arranged so that I could work on the RAMP application from the privacy of a basement office. I became hyper-focused. I prepared and overprepared in my search for the statistics and other pertinent information we needed.

Long story short: PSD is the first deaf school in the country to become a Recognized ASCA Model Program.

Fast forward a few years, and I'm reading Plumb's *The Satisfied Introvert.* His account of the methodical approach rings true. Not just the part where he rehearsed multiple times over multiple days to ace a grade school assignment, but other projects as well—both at school and in the workforce. He described this as his winning recipe.

Once again, this is exactly what I do. A winning recipe. It works for me.

But here's the catch. If you apply a methodical approach to something you enjoy, as I did with ASCA, it's fine. For an introvert, hyper-focusing on a project in the quiet solitude of a basement office is a welcome assignment.

Public speaking is an entirely different story. Sometimes I'm fine with it. There's a sense of purpose that comes with getting people to understand a deaf perspective. Other times, I have no interest in being on stage. I'd rather stay home. But for whatever reason, I can't say no. And then I find myself on stage suppressing an anxiety attack.

In either scenario—welcome challenge or unwanted source of stress—I usually do a good job, thanks to my tendency to overprepare. And because I do well—regardless of whether I enjoyed it or not—I find myself being asked to do it again. I've had trouble turning down presentations because the extroverted world has often made me feel like it's *something I'm supposed to do.*

My sense of humor—which you've seen in this book—can also be a winning recipe, for better and for worse. I love joking around. Sometimes I do it because I'm genuinely having fun. Sometimes I do it because I'm masking the pain of an unpleasant situation. And somehow, I always seem to find myself back in the very same unpleasant situation, over and over.

This is exactly what Plumb warns about in *The Satisfied Introvert.* The danger of having a winning recipe is that you run the risk of building a facade. A facade where you give everyone the impression that everything's okay when it's actually not. You may be creating a barrier—perhaps even a false identity—where your interaction with others is inauthentic.

Here's the paradigm shift: I spent the first 23 years of my life pretending to be a hearing person. Understanding this helped me become more self-aware as a deaf adult. But this is just one facet of my life. Plumb's writing made me realize that I had spent the first 56 years of my life pretending to be an extrovert. It was a mind-blowing *a-ha!* moment.

Omigod! I can't believe I missed that!

If you make it look like everything is okay while you're burning the candle at both ends, you set yourself up for more of the same. Extroverts have no idea how hard you work to fit in with their world. You're doing what comes naturally to them. If you successfully pull it off, they'll expect you to do it again. Next thing you know, you have an introvert hangover.

This is yet another parallel with the deaf experience. The social bluffing that deaf people are known to do? It's a facade we feel obligated to put on in order to fit in with the predominantly hearing world. When we do this, the hearing folks don't realize what we're actually going through. Then they expect us to keep doing it, and the cycle continues. They're less inclined to take us seriously when we request accommodations because we "look just like any other normal hearing person."

I've learned from this. These days, I tell people straight up that I'm an introvert (which is precisely what Plumb says we're supposed to do). Now I get more opportunities to do things from a position of strength.

I highly recommend checking out Plumb's website—thesatisfiedintrovert.com—for more information on how you can do the same.

When I do venture out of my comfort zone, I still overprepare as a means of gaining confidence. But *having confidence* means more freedom to do things my way. It also means speaking up when I stray a bit too far out of my comfort zone. Of course, sometimes I fall back into bad habits, such as forgetting it's okay to say no.

Plumb says we never really stop using our winning recipe. It's too ingrained. But we can lessen or remove the power it has over us when we detach from it and tell other people that we're introverts. When you're this open with people, they're more apt to recognize your strengths and respect your boundaries.

Be comfortable with who you are and let people know how you roll. Everyone has their own way of reaching their goals.

Extrovert: Hmmm. I have an idea. Let me run it by everyone at the staff meeting.

Introvert: Hmmm. I have an idea. Let me go for a walk.

Neither approach is wrong. Both of these guys are going to wind up with a solid plan. Do whatever works best for you. As Plumb wisely put it: "You cannot be a satisfied introvert until you feel secure as an introvert."

THE CHEAT CODE

If you're an introvert, you've probably said *that's exactly how I feel* multiple times already. Those of you who are extroverts may have said *so that's why I have to drag Larry kicking and screaming to poker night.*

Although there are tips on how to survive the awkward moments we inevitably face in the extrovert world, it doesn't mean you have to put on an extrovert mask. To be yourself is the biggest gift you can give to the world.

It's also the biggest gift you can give to yourself.

Every chapter in this book has something that encourages you to be your authentic self. But it's not going to happen overnight. We say we're going to be our own person, only to find ourselves back in the same people-pleasing mode we thought we swore off. It's like going to a family reunion and feeling like you're eight years old again.

Here's a condensed cheat code that can help you stay on track. You can refer back to it anytime you need.

- Tell people you're an introvert. It's that simple. That's thousands of misunderstandings nipped in the bud from the get-go. Especially if you have a Resting Bitch Face.

- Don't be shy about being an introvert, either. Tell it like it is. *"I'm an introvert. I would rather dump a thousand fire ants in my underwear than attend a class reunion."* Granted, being an introvert can feel awkward at times. But when you own it, the awkwardness goes away. More power to you.

- If you're in one of those elephant-in-the-room scenarios, pet the elephant. Nothing defuses tension better than acknowledging it's there.

- Never apologize for being an introvert. Reframe it as an actual identity with admirable traits (which it is). Don't perceive it as something that's "less than" an extrovert ideal.

- If you ever get the feeling that extroverts don't understand you, you're right. They don't. You might need to show them the science behind introversion before any of them get it. Study the contrasting effects of dopamine on introverts and extroverts, and be prepared to explain it. You'll be taken more seriously if you can do this.

- Be aware that there are some things you do that others might perceive as idiosyncrasies. For example, my need to get into *The Zone* before any public speaking event. It's not an idiosyncrasy. It's important to me. Not doing it causes actual mental and physical stress. The same thing happened with Professor Brian Little (as described in Susan Cain's *Quiet*). You know what works best for you. Defend your way of doing things. It's not silly at all.

- There are other introverts out there. They're at school, at work, and at social events. Find them. You'll have each other's backs like no one else can. Not sure who the introverts are? Scan the room whenever an icebreaking activity is announced. You'll know. And here's a paradox: *you'll never be alone when you know there are other people who want to be alone.*

- Find introverts online, too. Read their works and know that *it's not just you.* I'm a fan of the *Understanding Introverts* Facebook page and Jenn Granneman's *Introvert, Dear* online community. It's empowering.

- Go to Benjamin Plumb's *The Satisfied Introvert* website (thesatis-fiedintrovert.com) and do an honest self-assessment. You'll find yourself letting go of the *you shoulds* you may have internalized as an introvert living in an extroverted world. *Note: this is probably the most valuable suggestion in the whole book. Most self-help resources address symptoms. Plumb addresses the cause.*

- Recharge. Always recharge. Would you go on a 100-mile trip in an electric car that only has enough juice to go 25 miles? Of course not. The same thing applies to you.

- Whenever possible, have a sidekick when you're assigned intro-vert-draining tasks such as leading a workshop. Your energy will last longer. Or, if you have a solid relationship with your super-visor, say *"for chrissakes, don't put me in charge of something like that again."*

- That sidekick is great for getting you through unavoidable awk-ward situations. But when you're in your element and doing what you do best, such as working on a written report, fly solo. Sidekicks will save you in public but distract you in private. Find the right balance.

- Go on a comedy-watching binge every now and then. Develop a feel for delivery and timing. It'll come in handy when you least expect it.

- Multitasking is overrated. Focus on one thing at a time. Hy-per-focus. It's what we do best.

- Always make sure you have your steady allotment of alone time. If anyone objects, tell them it's intermittent fasting for the brain. It's good for you.

- Quiet moments of solitude lead to the best ideas. Write your ideas down. They could wind up becoming part of a great book, a captivating presentation, or a game-changer at work.

- When you've got something good going on, don't pop the bubble. Don't share your goals with others until you're absolutely certain they're going to come to fruition.

- Sometimes we feel awkward with others during inevitable moments of silence. Adjust your body language so that you look confident. Then allow yourself to *feel* confident. Have you ever been in a bad mood, but suddenly something made you smile? And then that bad mood faded away? A smile has that effect. So does your posture. The mind-body connection is a two-way street.

- If you feel socially awkward to the point where you want to ask for support, ask another introvert. They understand what you're going through better than anyone else.

- If you're socially awkward and don't care, we should have a beer sometime.

- If you absolutely dislike small talk, skip over it. Get right to the point. You'll be surprised at how many people actually appreciate this. You're being genuine.

- Be mindful of careers that are a good match for an introvert. Most likely you're on the *40 years then retire and die* plan. Do you want to spend those 40 years pretending to be someone you're not? Do you want to put on an extrovert mask every morning and then come home completely exhausted? Earlier in the book, we saw how Jim Henderson transferred to a department that matched his skills and personality. Be like Jim.

- Not a fan of the 40 Year Plan? Consider being an entrepreneur, then. Times are changing. You can do this online, from the comfort of your own home.

- Networking doesn't necessarily mean schmoozing in large crowds. Be the quality person you are in small groups and treat individuals with the utmost respect. Collectively, a large group will have a positive opinion of you even if you've never rubbed elbows with them in a crowded conference room.

- Not comfortable reaching out in person? Email is your friend. Got a great idea at work? Again, email it to everyone. An email is like a time-stamped copyright.

- Exercise regularly and maintain a good diet. Introverts tend to be stressed—and therefore more prone to anxiety—in extroverted environments. Exercise defuses stress. Find the kind of exercise that appeals to you no matter if it's a weightlifting session or a quiet walk through a park.

- Take a bath. Go outside. Read. Take a nap. Get a massage. Listen to music. Write poetry. Read poetry. Find quiet time. Draw or paint. Talk to a friend. Do crossword puzzles. Doesn't all of this sound cliché? It is! But you've got to grant yourself permission to do it. You're just as important as all of those people you're exhausting yourself for.

- The exercise and take a bath stuff are good for you. Obviously, they feel good and relieve stress. It helps to make that a regular routine. But be mindful of what's causing you stress in the first place. Can you reduce it?

- Be aware of what overstimulates you. If you like parties but can only hang out for two hours before your battery runs out, have a recharge plan (such as excusing yourself for an extended break) or an exit plan (all right, all right). If you don't like parties, don't go.

- If you don't like parties but staying home is not an option—good luck trying to bail out of your mother's 75th birthday—assign yourself a role that reduces unwanted interaction time. Camera guy. Bartender. Burger flipper. Annoying guy smoking a pipe. Whatever works.

- Prepare well in advance for any projects, presentations, or interviews. Have a pre-game routine that grounds you.

- If you find yourself doing any sort of public speaking, have a trusted friend or colleague who can help keep you anchored. If there isn't anyone available, connect with a member of the audience and build on that. Find your Uncle Fred.

- If you find yourself asking *why am I doing any sort of public speaking*, examine that. Did you agree to it out of a sense of obligation? Could you have said no? Was it a part of a job requirement? Could you have asked if it could have been delegated to someone else?

- Say no. Everyone seems to feel guilty about saying no. Don't. It's a form of self-respect.

- If you have to, use the *Say No Formula* to give yourself permission to say no: *hours of stuff you really wanted to do divided by hours awake times one hundred equals the percentage of time spent doing what's important to you.* The numbers don't lie.

- If people-pleasing is a habit that's hard to break, get a copy of Andrew Leedham's *Unstoppable Self Confidence.* You'll thank me later.

- If you pretend everything's okay, people will believe you. Be honest with yourself. Say something.

- Find creative ways to be assertive. You don't have to be Pat Croce and bang on doors. Use the power of the written word. Letters, emails, blogs, and social media are all effective tools to share your ideas.

- Make time for the hobbies and activities that you truly enjoy. Do them, and by virtue of doing what interests you, you become fully charged. People develop an appreciation for who you really are *when you take the time to be who you really are.*

- Create a goals-oriented PowerPoint. Don't just list things you want to do. Make it visible. Make slides with pictures of your dream vacation. When you look at them, *feel it*. On an exercise program? Create a slide with a picture of someone close to your age who has achieved the fitness goals you're aiming for. Look at that picture as if it's you. Again, *feel it.* As introverts, we easily get distracted by others; this exercise, done daily and in solitude, wires you to stay on track with your goals. And then they happen.

- This book is not *How to be an Introvert.* It's about embracing who you are. Take whatever information is useful and disregard the rest.

RECOMMENDED READING

When I started writing this book, I only intended to share my own personal experience as an introvert. Then I wound up adding stories of friends and coworkers who are also introverts, as a means of showing *it's not just me.*

To further emphasize *it's not just me,* I sought out other books by and about introverts. This was solely for the purpose of backing up what I wrote. I get a lot of *oh, come on, you're not really an introvert* so I looked for solid evidence that *oh, yes, I am.*

I thought these books would reinforce things that I already knew. But as I got absorbed in each one, I wound up learning so much about myself in ways that I never imagined. When I say that Jenn Granneman and Michaela Chung helped me repair relationships that were going down the toilet, it's no exaggeration.

Meanwhile, Benjamin Plumb showed up out of nowhere and got me to understand that my Introvert Self had almost exactly the same issues as my Deaf Self—but my Introvert Self was way behind in terms of self-awareness.

Mind blown.

There are also a couple of books listed here that technically aren't about introverts. They offer lessons in personal growth that help us immensely as we strive to be our authentic selves. As introverts, we often burn ourselves out trying to live up to extroverted ideals, so it helps to have resources that encourage you to be true to yourself.

While the following resources are books, keep an eye out for websites, too. There are too many to mention. My favorites are *Introvert, Dear* (introvertdear.com), *Introvert Spring* (introvertspring.com), and *The Satisfied Introvert* (thesatisfiedintrovert.com).

We never stop learning. Seek out more books. It's easier to help people understand you when you understand yourself. And please do understand that *it's not just you.* Our introvert world is very real, and we can thrive in it.

Without any further ado, here's my recommended reading list.

- *Quiet: The Power of Introverts in a World That Can't Stop Talking* by Susan Cain (Crown Publishing Group / Random House, Inc., 2012)

- *The Introvert Advantage: How Quiet People Can Thrive in an Extrovert World* by Marti Olsen Laney, Psy.D. (Workman Publishing Company, 2002)

- *The Introverted Leader: Building on Your Quiet Strength* by Jennifer B. Kahnweiler, Ph.D. (Berrett-Koehler Publishers, 2013)

- *Quiet Influence: The Introvert's Guide to Making a Difference* by Jennifer B. Kahnweiler, Ph.D. (Berrett-Koehler Publishers, 2013)

- *The Secret Lives of Introverts: Inside our Hidden World* by Jenn Granneman (Skyhorse, 2017)

- *The Irresistible Introvert: Harness the Power of Quiet Charisma in a Loud World* by Michaela Chung (Skyhorse, 2016)

- *Introvert Power: Why Your Inner Life is Your Hidden Strength* by Laurie Helgoe, Ph.D. (Sourcebooks, 2008)

- *The Satisfied Introvert: A Memoir About Finding Safety in an Extroverted World* by Benjamin Plumb (The Satisfied Introvert LLC, 2022)

- *Burnout: The Secret to Unlocking the Stress Cycle* by Emily Nagoski, Ph.D. and Amelia Nagoski, DMA (Ballantine Books, 2019)

- *Reinvent Yourself* by James Altucher (Choose Yourself Media, 2017)

- *Unstoppable Self Confidence: How to Create the Indestructable, Natural Confidence of the 1% Who Achieve Their Goals, Create Success on Demand and Live Life on Their Terms* by Andrew Leedham (Unstoppable Media Group, Ltd, 2019)

ACKNOWLEDGMENTS

To Melanie, Darren, Brandon, Lacey, and Sherry. You're the best family a guy could ask for. Thank you for being so accepting of a writer dad and all of the quirks that come with the territory. On top of that, each one of you has overcome adversity in a way that makes me greatly appreciate you. I'm truly humbled and love you so much.

To Joshua Sprague. My fingers can't stop typing ever since I took your course. Thank you for showing that the impossible is possible.

To Victoria Davidson and the entire team at Killer Covers. No matter how many times I slowed down this project with my over-thinking, you went ahead and demonstrated the most impressive creativity and innovation I have ever seen. Thank you so much.

To Benjamin Plumb. Your words set off a chain reaction of *a-ha!* moments that had a profound impact. Your ability to empower in-troverts with heightened self-awareness is much appreciated.

ABOUT THE AUTHOR

Mark Drolsbaugh has accomplished a thing or two here and there. He isn't fond of filling out "about the author" blurbs because he knows most people glaze over them. Seriously, why bother? He's an introvert. He spends most of his time with his wife, kids, dog, and cats. When he's not doing that, he's probably reading a book. Or watching TV. Who knows? Sometimes he'll go out. He'll hang out with a few friends at a local watering hole. Then he'll disappear for a couple of months. Those who understand this smile knowingly and look forward to next time, whenever that may be.

Made in the USA
Middletown, DE
09 August 2023